Crocheted Bees, Bugs & Butterflies

Crocheted Bees, Bugs & Butterflies

VANESSA MOONCIE

Contents

Introduction

I have always been interested in nature and find insects particularly compelling. The colour and pattern in these creatures are inspiring. They look like beautiful, delicate jewels. I enjoy working on a small scale and wanted to create a selection of detailed crocheted miniature beasts.

This book is a collection of 10 projects, including a selection of swallowtail butterflies, a stag beetle, a praying mantis and a cicada. Four of the insects have instructions for variations on the designs, to make different species or colourways.

Fine yarns and threads, and a variety of crochet stitches and colourwork, are used for shaping and defining the patterns and features. The majority of each piece is crocheted in cotton. The addition of fluffy alpaca yarn and metallic embroidery thread give the projects interesting texture and sparkle. Craft wire is used for the foundation of legs and antennae, as well as to give a couple of the bodies a rigid form. Glass beads, sequins and simple embroidery complete the projects.

All the projects have charts to accompany the written instructions to make it easy to follow the patterns. At the back of the book there are illustrated step-by-step instructions on the crochet stitches, working in multiple colours and adding the finishing touches. There is also information on mounting the finished pieces for display, or turning them into wearable accessories.

Vanessa Mooncie

Note: These pieces are not suitable for small children, as each one has wire worked into one or more parts of the body.

Bumblebees

page 24

Cicada
page 32

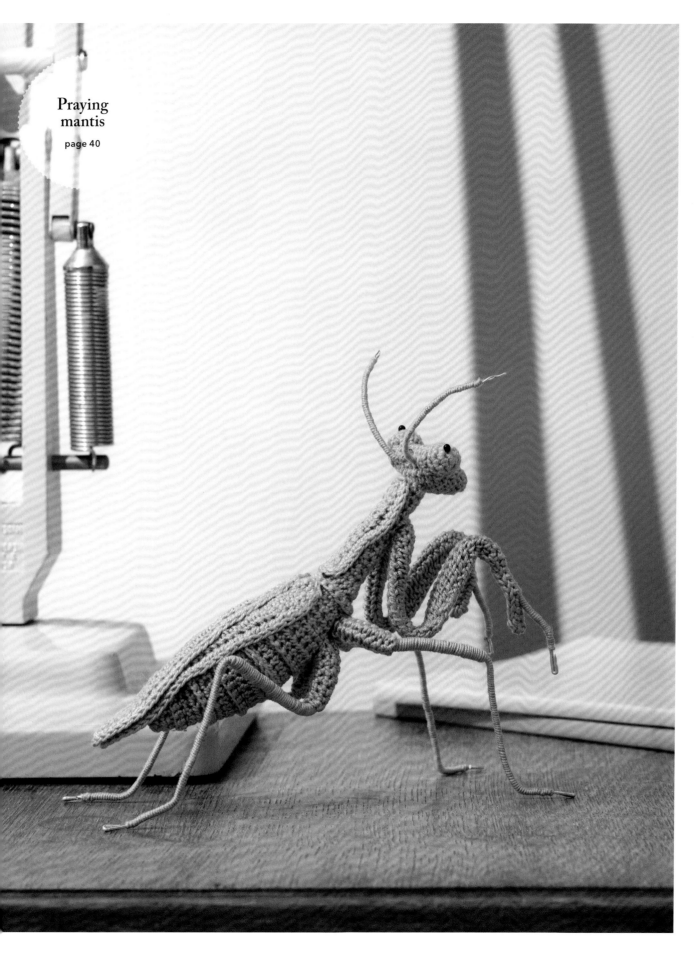

Praying
mantis
page 40

Christmas
beetle

page 52

Tiger
swallowtail
butterfly
page 63

Zebra
swallowtail
butterfly
page 68

Pipevine
swallowtail
butterfly
page 72

Dragonfly
page 76

Ladybird

page 84

Mirror
spider
page 92

Moths
page 98

Stag beetle

page 112

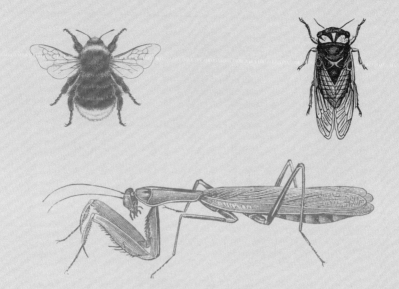

Projects

Bumblebees

Each bumblebee uses only a small amount
of yarn, so there will be enough to start a colony
or make a few different species.

Materials

♦ Drops Kid-Silk uni-colour, 75% mohair,
25% silk (230yd/210m per 25g ball):

White-tailed bumblebee

1 x 25g ball in 02 Black (A)
1 x 25g ball in 30 Curry (B)
1 x 25g ball in 01 Off-White (C)

Red-tailed bumblebee

1 x 25g ball in 02 Black (A)
1 x 25g ball in 33 Rust (B)

Tree bumblebee

1 x 25g ball in 02 Black (A)
1 x 25g ball in 42 Almond (B)
1 x 25g ball in 01 Off-White (C)

All bees

♦ Metallic stranded embroidery thread, such as DMC
Light Effects, shade E436, for the wings
♦ 1.25mm (UK3:US8) crochet hooks
♦ Blunt-ended darning needle
♦ Small amount of toy stuffing

♦ 4 lengths of 26-gauge (0.4mm) craft wire,
each measuring 6in (15cm), for the wings
♦ 3 lengths of 26-gauge (0.4mm) craft wire,
each measuring 4¾in (12cm), for the legs
♦ 1 pair of ³⁄₁₆in (5mm) rice or barrel beads for the eyes
♦ Clear nylon invisible thread
♦ Long-nose pliers
♦ All-purpose adhesive

Size

Approximately 1⅝in (4cm) long, excluding antennae
and legs.

Tension

38 sts and 40 rows to 4in (10cm) over double crochet
using 1.25mm hook and A. Use larger or smaller
hook if necessary to obtain correct tension.

Method

The bumblebee's head, thorax and abdomen are crocheted in one piece, in continuous rounds of double crochet. The wings are crocheted with a single strand of metallic embroidery thread. Openwork in various stitches creates the delicate pattern. The last round is crocheted around wire. The wings are stitched to the thorax. The legs are made of craft wire wrapped in yarn and bent into shape after sewing them to the underside of the thorax. The bumblebee is finished with beads for the eyes and a short length of yarn sewn to the front of the head for the antennae.

1 ch at beg of the round does not count as a st throughout.

White-tailed bumblebee

Body

Head

With 1.25mm hook and A, make a magic loop (see page 127).
Round 1: 1 ch (does not count as a stitch), 6 dc into loop, turn (6 sts).
Round 2 (inc): (Dc2inc, 1 dc) 3 times (9 sts).
Pull tightly on short end of yarn to close loop.
Round 3: 1 dc in each dc.

Thorax

Round 4 (inc): (Dc2inc) 9 times (18 sts). Join B in last dc. Carry unused yarn on the WS of the work (see page 131).
Round 5: 1 dc in next 9 dc with B, 1 dc in next 9 dc with A.
Rounds 6–10: 1 dc in each dc with A.

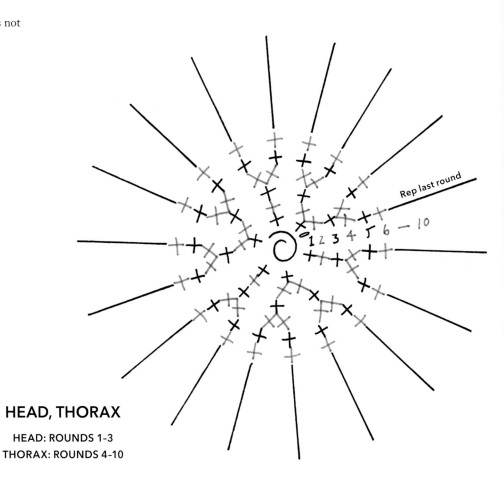

HEAD, THORAX

HEAD: ROUNDS 1-3
THORAX: ROUNDS 4-10

Abdomen

Round 11 (inc): (2 dc, dc2inc)
6 times (24 sts).
Rounds 12–13: 1 dc in next 15 dc
with B, 1 dc in next 9 dc with A.
Rounds 14–15: 1 dc in each dc
with A.
Round 16 (dec): (Dc2tog, 2 dc)
6 times (18 sts). Join C in last dc.
Round 17: 1 dc in each dc with C.
Round 18 (dec): (Dc2tog, 1 dc)
6 times (12 sts).
Round 19: 1 dc in each dc.
Fasten off, leaving a long tail of
yarn C.

ABDOMEN

ROUNDS 11-19

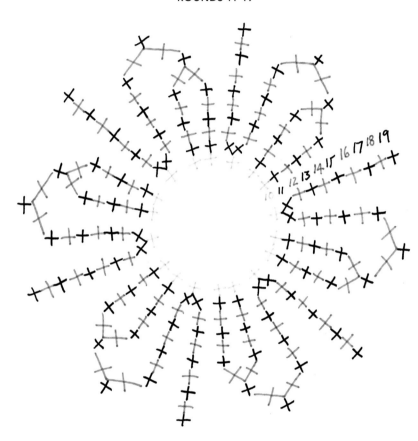

Key

◠	Magic loop	✕✕	dc2inc
⟋	Chain (ch)	✕✕	dc2tog
•	Slip stitch (sl st)	T	Half treble (htr)
+	Double crochet (dc)	Ŧ	Treble (tr)

Forewings (make 2)

With 1.25mm hook and one strand of embroidery thread, make 12 ch.
Round 1: 1 dc in 2nd ch from hook, 1 dc in next 3 ch, 2 ch, skip 2 ch, 1 htr in next 2 ch, 2 ch, skip 2 ch, 5 tr in end ch, 2 ch, skip 2 ch, 1 htr in reverse side of next 2 ch, 2 ch, skip 2 ch, 1 dc in reverse side of next 4 ch (17 sts and 4 2-ch sps).
Do not fasten off.

Forewing edging

Round 2: Working around the craft wire, 1 dc in next 4 dc, 2 dc in next 2-ch sp, 1 dc in next 2 htr, 2 dc in next 2-ch sp, 2 dc in next 5 tr, 2 dc in next 2-ch sp, 1 dc in next 2 htr, 2 dc in next 2-ch sp, 1 dc in next 4 dc, sl st to first st (30 sts).
Fasten off, leaving a long tail of thread.

**FOREWINGS
FOREWING EDGING**

**FOREWINGS: ROUND 1
FOREWING EDGING: ROUND 2**

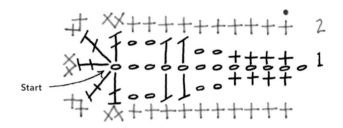

Hindwings (make 2)

With 1.25mm hook and one strand
of embroidery thread, make 8 ch.
Round 1: 1 dc in 2nd ch from hook,
1 dc in next 3 ch, 2 ch, skip 2 ch,
5 htr in end ch, 2 ch, skip 2 ch, 1 dc
in reverse side of next 4 ch (13 sts and
2 2-ch sps).
Do not fasten off.

Hindwing edging

Round 2: Working around the craft
wire, 1 dc in next 4 dc, 2 dc in next
2-ch sp, 2 dc in next 5 htr, 2 dc in
next 2-ch sp, 1 dc in next 4 dc,
sl st to first st (22 sts).
Fasten off, leaving a long tail
of thread.

**HINDWINGS,
HINDWING EDGING**

HINDWINGS: ROUND 1
HINDWING EDGING: ROUND 2

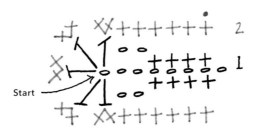

Red-tailed bumblebee

Body

Head
Rounds 1–3: Work as for white-tailed bumblebee.

Thorax
Rounds 4–10: Work as for white-tailed bumblebee using A throughout.

Abdomen
Rounds 11–16 (dec): Work as for white-tailed bumblebee using A throughout.
Join B in last dc.
Rounds 17–19: Work as for white-tailed bumblebee using B. Fasten off, leaving a long tail of yarn B.

Tree bumblebee

Body

Head
Rounds 1–3: Work as for white-tailed bumblebee.

Thorax
Rounds 4–5: Work as for white-tailed bumblebee.
Rounds 6–10: Rep round 5.

Abdomen
Rounds 11–16 (dec): Work as for white-tailed bumblebee using A throughout.
Join C in last dc.
Rounds 17–19: Work as for white-tailed bumblebee.
Fasten off, leaving a long tail of yarn C.

Making up

Body

Stuff the body, keeping the base flat. Thread a tail of yarn through the last round of the body and pull up tightly to close.

Legs

Follow the instructions for the antennae on page 135 to make three pairs of legs, wrapping the wire with A. Make two bends on each side of the covered wire to shape the legs and sew to the base of the body using A.

Wings

Trim the excess wire on the wings to within ⅛in (3mm). Use pliers to bend under the sharp ends. Pull each wing gently so the bent ends of the wire disappear just inside the stitches. Place one of the forewings on top of one of the hindwings and, using the tail of thread left after fastening off, sew the lower ends together. Do the same for the second set of wings. Sew the wings to the thorax.

Eyes

Attach the beads vertically to the head using invisible thread (see page 135). Weave the threads from one side of the head to the other and pull tightly to pinch the head into shape before fastening off.

Antennae

Sew a length of A to the front of the head, between the eyes. Trim excess yarn.

Weave in all the yarn ends.

Cicada

This design is based on the periodical cicada. A combination of cotton and metallic threads are used for this project. The colours can be changed to make different species of cicada.

Materials

- Anchor Freccia, 100% cotton (311yd/285m per 50g ball): 1 x 50g ball in 00403 (A)
- Metallic stranded embroidery thread, such as Anchor Lamé, shade 318, for the wings
- Stranded embroidery thread, such as Anchor Stranded Cotton, shade 340, for the legs
- 1.50mm (UK2½:US7) and 1.75mm (UK2:US6) crochet hooks
- Sharp-ended darning needle
- Small amount of toy stuffing
- 2 lengths of 26-gauge (0.4mm) craft wire, each measuring 8in (20cm), for the wings
- 3 lengths of 26-gauge (0.4mm) craft wire, each measuring 6in (15cm), for the legs
- 1 pair of ⁵⁄₃₂in (4mm) red glass beads
- 3 size 11/0, ¹⁄₁₆in (2mm) black seed beads
- Clear nylon invisible thread
- Long-nose pliers
- All-purpose adhesive
- PVA glue

Size

Approximately 2¾in (7cm) long, excluding antennae and legs.

Tension

34 sts and 33 rows to 4in (10cm) over double crochet using 1.75mm hook. Use larger or smaller hook if necessary to obtain correct tension.

Method

The cicada's head, pronotum, thorax and abdomen are crocheted in one piece, in a combination of continuous rounds and rows of double crochet. A line of stitches crocheted into unworked loops of a previous round forms the mesonotum and an edging at the front and back of the pronotum. The mesonotum and pronotum are both sections of the cicada's thorax. The wings are crocheted with two strands of metallic embroidery thread. A variety of stitches, with chain spaces between, creates the openwork pattern. The last round is crocheted around wire. The legs are made of craft wire wrapped in embroidery thread and bent into shape. The cicada is finished with coloured beads for the compound eyes, seed beads for the small eyes and a short length of crochet thread sewn to the front of the head for the antennae.

1 ch at beg of the row/round does not count as a st throughout.

Body

Head

With 1.75mm hook and A, make a magic loop (see page 127).
Round 1: 1 ch, 6 dc into loop (6 sts).
Round 2 (inc): (Dc2inc) 6 times (12 sts).
Round 3: 1 dc in each dc.
Round 4 (inc): (Dc2inc) 6 times, 1 dc in next 6 dc (18 sts).

Pronotum

The following is worked in rows.
Row 1 (RS): 1 dc in back loop only of next 12 dc, 1 dc in both loops of next 6 dc, turn.
Row 2 (WS): 1 ch, 1 dc in each dc, turn.
Row 3 (dec): Working in back loops only, (1 dc, dc2tog) twice, (dc2tog, 1 dc) twice, 1 dc in both loops of next 6 dc, turn (14 sts).
Row 4 (inc): 1 dc in both loops of next 6 dc; working in front loops only, (1 dc, dc2inc) twice, (dc2inc, 1 dc) twice, turn (18 sts).

HEAD

ROUNDS 1-4

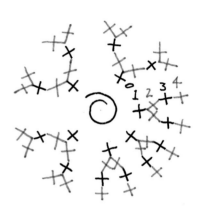

Thorax

Rows 5–6: 1 ch, 1 dc in each dc, turn.
Row 7: 1 ch, 1 dc in each dc. Do not turn.

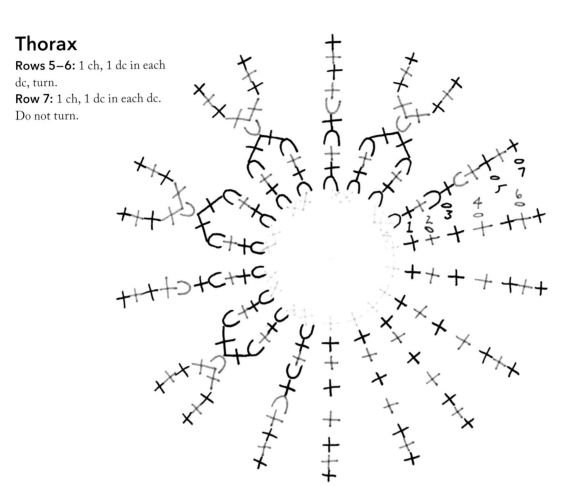

PRONOTUM, THORAX

PRONOTUM: ROWS 1-4
THORAX: ROWS 5-7

Key

↺	Magic loop		⊤	Half treble (htr)
⟋	Chain (ch)		⟊	Treble (tr)
•	Slip stitch (sl st)		⟊	Double treble (dtr)
+	Double crochet (dc)		⥾	dtr2inc
⤬	dc2inc		∩	work into back loop only
⤬	dc3inc		∪	work into front loop only
⤬	dc2tog			

Abdomen

The following is worked in continuous rounds.

Rounds 1–3: 1 dc in each dc.

Round 4 (dec): (Dc2tog, 1 dc) 6 times (12 sts).

Round 5: 1 dc in each dc.

Round 6 (dec): (Dc2tog, 2 dc) 3 times (9 sts).

Round 7: 1 dc in each dc.

Round 8 (dec): (Dc2tog, 1 dc) 3 times (6 sts).

Fasten off, leaving a long tail of thread.

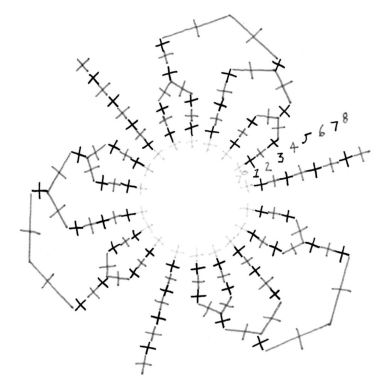

ABDOMEN

ROUNDS 1-8

Mesonotum

With head facing downwards and 1.75mm hook, join A with a sl st to the first of 8 unworked back loops of row 3 of pronotum.

Row 1 (RS): 1 dc in unworked loop of next st, (1 htr, 1 tr) in next st, (dtr2inc) twice, (1 tr, 1 htr) in next st, 1 dc in next st, sl st in next st, turn (10 sts).

Row 2 (WS): 1 dc in next dc, 1 dc in next 9 sts, sl st in same loop as sl st.

Row 3: Rep row 2.

Fasten off, leaving a long tail of thread.

MESONOTUM

ROWS 1-3

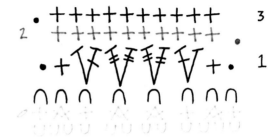

Pronotum edging

Front

Next: With head facing downwards, 1.75mm hook and A, sl st in each of 12 unworked front loops of round 4 of head.

Fasten off, leaving a long tail of thread.

PRONOTUM EDGING

FRONT

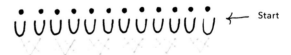

Back

Next: With head facing upwards, 1.75mm hook, sl st in first of 12 unworked front loops of row 2 of pronotum, 1 dc in same st as sl st, 1 dc in next 11 sts.

Fasten off, leaving a long tail of thread.

PRONOTUM EDGING

BACK

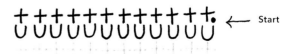

Wings (make 2)

With 1.50mm hook and two strands of metallic embroidery thread, make 16 ch.

Round 1: 1 dc in 2nd ch from hook, 1 dc in next 2 ch, (2 ch, skip 2 ch, 1 htr in next ch) 3 times, 2 ch, skip 2 ch, (1 htr, 2 ch, 1 htr, 3 ch, 1 tr, 3 ch, 1 dtr, 4 ch, 1 dtr) in end ch; working in reverse side of each ch, 4 ch, skip 2 ch, 1 tr in next ch, (3 ch, skip 2 ch, 1 htr in next ch) twice, 3 ch, skip 2 ch, 1 dc in next 3 ch to finish lower part of wing (17 sts and 12 ch sps).
Do not fasten off.

Wing edging

Round 2: Working around the craft wire, 2 dc in next dc, 1 dc in next 2 dc, (2 dc in next 2-ch sp, 1 dc in next htr) 5 times, 3 dc in next 3-ch sp, 1 dc in next tr, 3 dc in next 3-ch sp, dc3inc in next dtr, 4 dc in next 4-ch sp, 1 dc in next dtr, 4 dc in next 4-ch sp, 1 dc in next tr, (3 dc in next 3-ch sp, 1 dc in next htr) twice, 3 dc in next 3-ch sp, 1 dc in next 2 dc, dc2inc, sl st to first dc (54 sts).
Fasten off, leaving a long tail of thread.

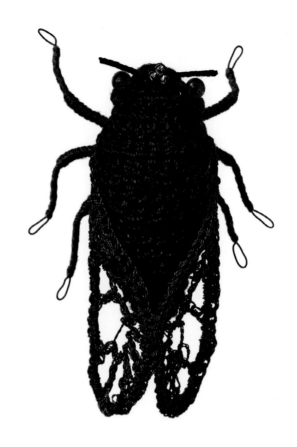

WINGS, WING EDGING

WINGS: ROUND 1
WING EDGING: ROUND 2

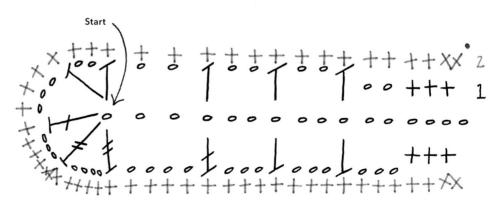

Making up

Body

Stuff the body, keeping the base flat. Sew together the open edges at the side of the body. Use a tail of thread left after fastening off the mesonotum to sew the edges to the surface of the body. Sew the corners of the edging on the front and back of the pronotum to the body, using the tails of thread left after fastening off.

Legs

Follow instructions for the antennae on page 135 to make three pairs of legs. Wind three strands of embroidery thread around the twisted wire, starting at the looped end of one leg and working over the end of the thread to the middle. Wind a second layer in the opposite direction back over the wrapped wire to within ¾in (2cm) from the end. Wind a third layer back to the centre. Take the thread to the end of the other leg and repeat to cover the other side in the same way. Trim the excess thread and secure the end of the thread with a dab of all-purpose adhesive and allow to dry. Bend the legs to shape and sew them to the base of the body using the same embroidery thread used to cover the wire.

Wings

Trim the excess wire on the wings to within ⅛in (3mm). Use pliers to bend under the sharp ends. Pull the wing gently so the bent ends of the wire disappear just inside the stitches.

Sew the wings behind the back edging of the pronotum, stitching neatly around the tops of the wings to attach them securely. Sew together two or three stitches at the top edges of the wings.

Eyes

For the compound eyes, sew the red beads to each side of the head using invisible thread (see page 135). For the ocelli, or simple eyes, sew three seed beads to the centre of the head, between the compound eyes, with invisible thread.

Antennae

Sew a length of A to the front of the head, between the eyes. Trim excess yarn. Apply a dab of PVA glue to the ends to prevent the yarn from fraying.

Weave in all the thread ends.

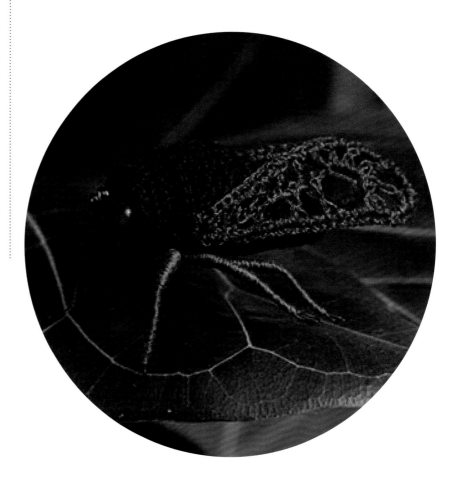

Praying mantis

Unworked loops of stitches are crocheted into to create raised lines across the surface, defining the segments of the praying mantis's abdomen. Seed beads are used for the pseudopupils in the crocheted compound eyes.

Materials

- ◆ Scheepjes Maxi Sweet Treat, 100% cotton (153yd/140m per 25g ball):
  1 x 25g ball in 513 Spring Green (A)
  1 x 25g ball in 245 Green Yellow (B)
- ◆ 1.25mm (UK3:US8) crochet hook
- ◆ Sharp-ended darning needle
- ◆ Small amount of toy stuffing
- ◆ 4¾in (12cm) length of 18-gauge (1mm) craft wire for the body
- ◆ 2 lengths of 18-gauge (1mm) craft wire, each measuring 9in (23cm), for the forelegs and hindlegs
- ◆ 8¼in (21cm) length of 18-gauge (1mm) craft wire for the middle legs
- ◆ 2 lengths of 26-gauge (0.4mm) craft wire, each measuring 9in (23cm), for the wings
- ◆ 8in (20cm) length of 26-gauge (0.4mm) craft wire for the antennae
- ◆ 3 size 11/0, ¹⁄₁₆in (2mm) green seed beads for the small eyes
- ◆ 2 size 11/0, ¹⁄₁₆in (2mm) black seed beads for the pseudopupils
- ◆ Clear nylon invisible thread
- ◆ Long-nose pliers
- ◆ All-purpose adhesive

Size

Approximately 5⅛in (13cm) long.

Tension

42 sts and 44 rows to 4in (10cm) over double crochet using 1.25mm hook. Use larger or smaller hook if necessary to obtain correct tension.

Method

The abdomen and thorax of the praying mantis are worked in rows of double crochet. Only one loop of each stitch is worked every few rows, so the unworked loops can be crocheted into to form the segments of the abdomen. The edging of the thorax is worked in the same way. Wire is inserted into the thorax, along with the stuffing, to keep its shape. The top piece of the thorax is made separately and sewn on after the body is stuffed. The wings are worked in rows using various stitches to create the shaping. The last round is crocheted around wire. The legs are made of craft wire, wrapped in yarn and finished with a crocheted piece to define the shaping. The legs are sewn to the body and bent into shape. The head and compound eyes are crocheted in rounds. The antennae are made with thinner wire than the legs and wrapped in yarn. The head is stuffed and the antennae is inserted inside the opening at the top of the head. The stitches on each side of the last round are sewn together with the centre of the antennae tucked inside the head. The compound eyes are sewn to the head. Seed beads are used for the three small eyes between the antennae and the pseudopupils in the compound eyes.

1 ch at beg of the row/round does not count as a st throughout.

Body

Abdomen

With 1.25mm hook and A, make 16 ch.
Row 1 (RS): 1 dc in 2nd ch from hook, 1 dc in each ch to end, turn (15 sts).
Row 2 (WS): 1 ch, 1 dc in each dc to end, turn.
Rows 3–4: Rep row 2.
Row 5 (inc): 1 ch, (1 dc, dc2inc, 1 dc) 5 times, turn (20 sts).
Rows 6–8: Rep row 2.
Row 9 (inc): 1 ch, (dc2inc, 3 dc) in back loops only 5 times, turn (25 sts).
Rows 10–11: Rep row 2.
Row 12: 1 ch, 1 dc in front loop only of each dc, turn.
Rows 13–14: Rep row 2.

Row 15 (dec): 1 ch, (dc2tog, 3 dc) in back loops only 5 times, turn (20 sts).
Rows 16–17: Rep row 2.
Row 18 (dec): 1 ch, (dc2tog, 2 dc) in front loops only 5 times, turn (15 sts).
Rows 19–20: Rep row 2.
Row 21 (dec): 1 ch, (dc2tog, 1 dc) in back loops only 5 times, turn (10 sts).
Rows 22–23: Rep row 2.
Row 24 (dec): 1 ch, (dc2tog) 5 times (5 sts).
Fasten off, leaving a long tail of yarn.

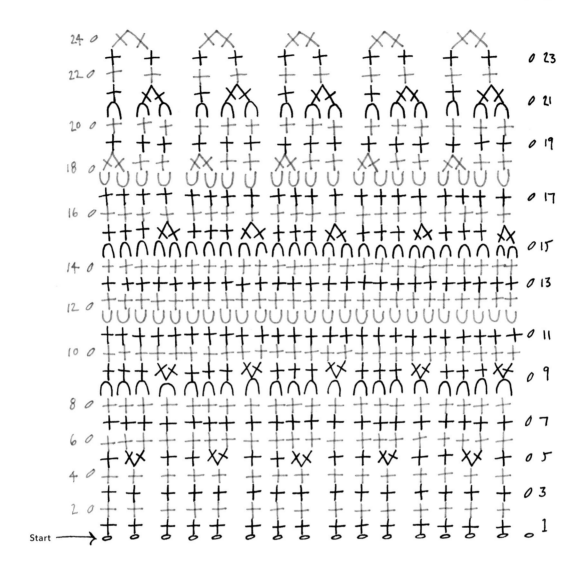

ABDOMEN

ROWS 1-24

Key

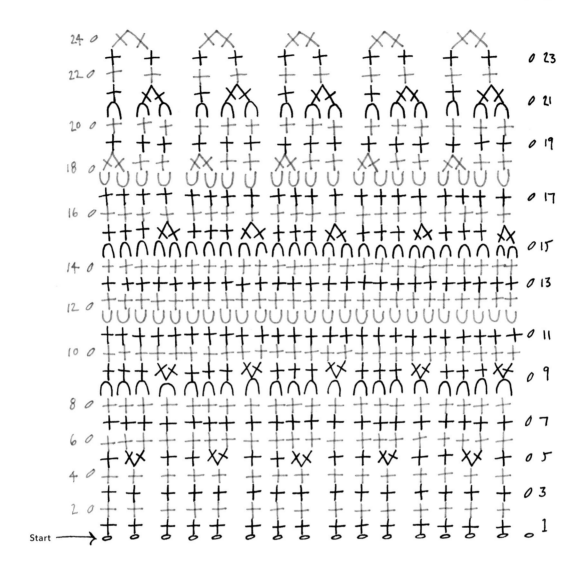

↻ Magic loop	✗✗ dc2tog
◌ Chain (ch)	⊤ Half treble (htr)
• Slip stitch (sl st)	⋁ htr2inc
✛ Double crochet (dc)	⊤ Treble (tr)
✗✗ dc2inc	∩ work into back loop only
✗✛✗ dc3inc	∪ work into front loop only

Thorax

With WS of abdomen facing and
1.25mm hook, join A with a sl st to
reverse side of first ch.

Row 1 (WS): 1 dc in same st as sl st,
1 dc in reverse side of each ch to end,
turn (15 sts).

Row 2 (RS) (dec): 1 ch, working in
back loops only, 1 dc in next 5 dc,
dc2tog, 1 dc in next dc, dc2tog,
1 dc in next 5 dc, turn (13 sts).

Row 3 (dec): 1 ch, 1 dc in next 4 dc,
dc2tog, 1 dc in next dc, dc2tog,
1 dc in next 4 dc, turn (11 sts).

Row 4 (dec): 1 ch, 1 dc in next 3 dc,
dc2tog, 1 dc in next dc, dc2tog,
1 dc in next 3 dc, turn (9 sts).

Row 5 (dec): 1 ch, 1 dc in next 2 dc,
dc2tog, 1 dc in next dc, dc2tog,
1 dc in next 2 dc, turn (7 sts).

Rows 6–17: 1 ch, 1 dc in each dc
to end, turn.

Row 18: 1 ch, 1 dc in back loop only
of each dc.

Fasten off, leaving a long tail of yarn.

Thorax edging

Next: With thorax facing upwards
and 1.25mm hook, sl st in first of
unworked front loops of row 1 of
thorax. Beg in same st as sl st,
1 dc in each unworked loop to end.
Fasten off.

THORAX

ROWS 1-17

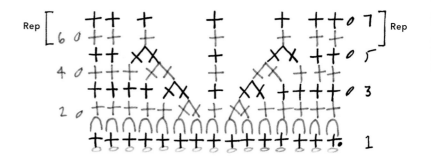

ROW 18

THORAX EDGING

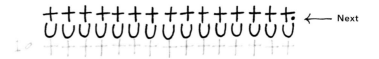

Next

ABDOMEN SEGMENTS

ROW 1

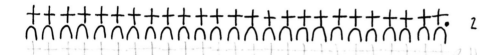

1

ROW 2

2

ROW 3

3

ROW 4

4

Abdomen segments

Row 1: *With thorax facing upwards and 1.25mm hook, sl st in first of unworked loops of row 8 of abdomen. Beg in same st as sl st, 1 dc in each unworked loop to end.
Fasten off.
Rows 2–5: Rep from * to finish the abdomen segments on the unworked loops of rows 11, 14, 17 and 20.

ROW 5

5

Top of thorax

With 1.25mm hook and A,
make 13 ch.

Row 1 (WS): 1 dc in 2nd ch from
hook, 1 dc in next 2 ch, 1 htr in next
ch, 2 htr in next ch, 1 htr in next ch,
1 dc in next 5 ch, 4 dc in end ch;
working in reverse side of each ch,
1 dc in next 5 ch, 1 htr in next ch,
2 htr in next ch, 1 htr in next ch,
1 dc in next 3 ch, turn (28 sts).

Row 2 (RS): With B, 1 ch, dc2inc,
1 dc in next 11 sts, dc3inc, 1 dc in
next 2 dc, dc3inc, 1 dc in next 11 sts,
dc2inc, sl st to first dc (34 sts).
Fasten off, leaving a long tail of A.

Head

With 1.25mm hook and A,
make a magic loop (see page 127).

Round 1: 1 ch, 6 dc into loop (6 sts).

Round 2 (inc): (Dc2inc, 1 dc)
3 times (9 sts).

Round 3: 1 dc in each dc.

Round 4 (inc): (Dc2inc, 2 dc)
3 times (12 sts).

Round 5 (inc): (Dc2inc, 3 dc)
3 times (15 sts).

Round 6 (inc): (Dc2inc, 4 dc)
3 times (18 sts).

Rounds 7–10: 1 dc in each dc.
Fasten off, leaving a long tail of yarn.

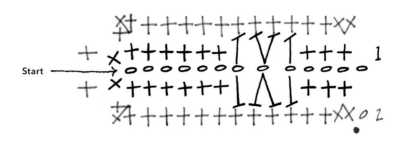

TOP OF THORAX

ROWS 1-2

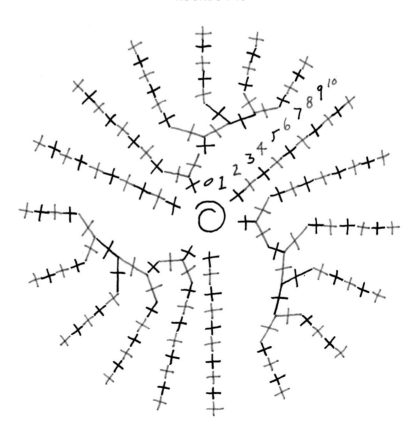

HEAD

ROUNDS 1-10

Eyes

With 1.25mm hook and B,
make a magic loop.
Round 1: 1 ch, 5 dc into loop (5 sts).
Round 2 (inc): (Dc2inc) 5 times.
Join A in last dc (10 sts).
Round 3: 1 dc in each dc.
Round 4: 1 dc in back loop only of
each dc, to finish the base of the eye.
Fasten off, leaving a long tail of A.

EYES

ROUNDS 1-4

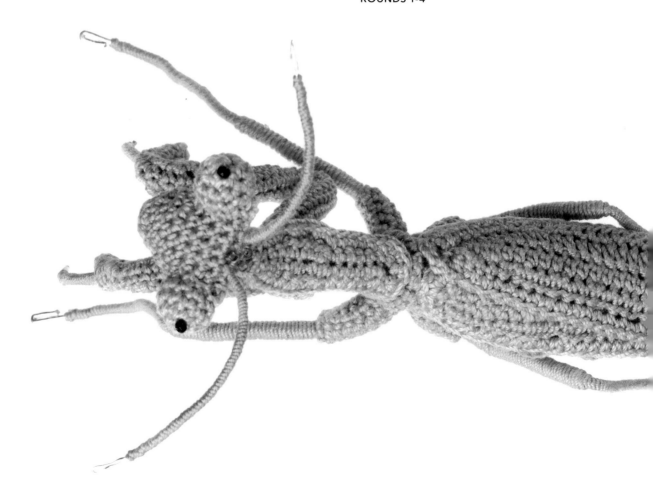

Wings (make 2)

With 1.25mm hook and A,
make 29 ch.
Row 1 (RS): 1 dc in 2nd ch from
hook, 1 dc in next ch, 1 htr in next
24 ch, 1 dc in next ch, 3 dc in end ch;
working in reverse side of each ch,
1 dc in next ch, 1 htr in next 24 ch,
1 dc in next ch, 2 dc in next ch,
turn (58 sts).
Row 2 (WS): 1 ch, (dc3inc, 1 dc in
next 5 sts, 1 htr in next 18 htr, 1 dc in
next 5 sts) twice, turn (62 sts).
Row 3: Working around the craft
wire with B, 1 ch, 1 dc in next 29 sts,
dc3inc, 1 dc in next 30 sts, dc3inc,
1 dc in next dc, sl st to first dc (66 sts).
Fasten off, leaving a long tail of A.

WINGS

ROWS 1-3

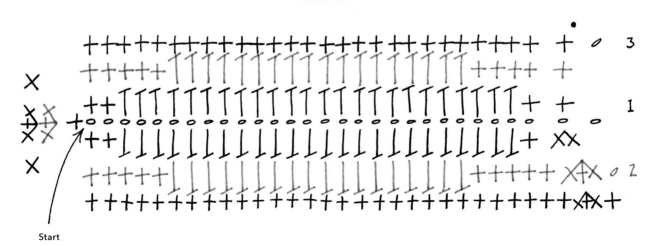

Start

Forelegs (make 2)

With 1.25mm hook and A,
make 42 ch.

Row 1 (RS): 1 dc in 2nd ch from
hook, 1 dc in each ch to end, 1 dc
in reverse side of each ch to end,
turn (82 sts).

Row 2 (WS): 2 ch, 1 htr in next 13
sts, sl st in next 2 sts, 1 dc in next st,
1 htr in next st, 1 tr in next 10 sts,
1 htr in next 3 sts, 1 dc in next st, sl st
in next 20 sts, 1 dc in next st, 1 htr in
next 3 sts, 1 tr in next 10 sts, 1 htr in
next st, 1 dc in next st, sl st in next 2
sts, 1 htr in next 13 sts, finishing at
the top of the leg.

Fasten off, leaving a long tail of yarn.

FORELEGS

ROWS 1-2

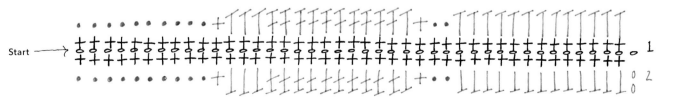

Middle and hind legs (make 2)

With 1.25mm hook and A, make 17 ch.

Row 1 (RS): 1 dc in 2nd ch from hook, 1 dc in next ch, 1 htr in next 12 ch, 1 dc in next 2 ch, turn (16 sts).
Row 2 (WS): 1 ch, 1 dc in each st to end, turn.
Row 3: Rep row 2.
Row 4: 1 ch, 1 dc in next 2 dc, 1 htr in next 12 dc, 1 dc in next 2 dc, turn. Fasten off, leaving a long tail of yarn.

Making up

Body

Thread a tail of yarn through the last round of the thorax and pull up tightly to close. Sew together the edges of the thorax. Thread the tail of yarn left after fastening off the abdomen through the last round and pull up tightly to close. Sew together the edges of the abdomen, leaving a gap to insert the wire and stuffing.

Use pliers to bend approximately ¼in (6mm) into a loop at each end of the wire and squeeze together. Bend the wire in the centre so the looped ends are together. Insert the wire, folded end first, through the opening and into the thorax.

Insert the looped ends inside the abdomen. Stuff the thorax, using the end of the crochet hook to push the stuffing to the end of the narrow neck, around the wire. Stuff the abdomen. Sew together the remaining stitches. The seams of the abdomen and thorax will run down the back of the praying mantis. Keep the back of the abdomen flat when stuffing.

With the tail of yarn left after fastening off, sew the top of the thorax piece down the length of the back of the thorax, positioning the wider part at the top and the narrow end just above the thorax edging.

Antennae

Follow instructions to make the antennae on page 135, wrapping the wire in yarn A.

Head

Stuff the head, keeping a flattened shape. Place antennae in the top of the head. Use the tail of yarn to sew together the nine stitches on each side of the last round, sewing the central three stitches on each side of the head together between the two antenna, enclosing the middle of the covered wire inside the head.

Eyes

Stuff the eyes. Thread the tail of yarn through the last round and pull up tightly to close, keeping the base flattened. Fasten off. Position the eyes towards the front of each side of the head, wrapping them towards the back of the head, so a portion of them can be seen from behind. Sew through the unworked loops of stitches around the base and into the head to attach them. For the small eyes, sew three green seed beads to the centre of the head, between the antennae, using invisible thread. Sew a black seed bead to each compound eye for the pseudopupils. Sew the head to the top of the thorax, stitching through the unworked loops at the top of the thorax and into the back of the head to attach it.

Forelegs

Use pliers to bend back approximately ¼in (6mm) from each end of the wire and squeeze together to make the feet. Starting at the foot, wind yarn A tightly around the wire, working over the yarn end, for approximately 1⅝in (4cm). Secure the end of the yarn with a dab of all-purpose adhesive and allow to dry. Repeat on the other end of the wire. Sew together the wide ends of the crocheted pieces to make one long

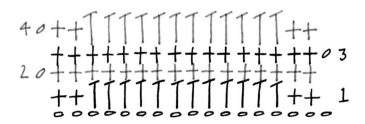

MIDDLE AND HIND LEGS

ROWS 1-4

strip. Lay the wire down the centre of the WS of the forelegs. Poke each foot through the fifth ch from the end of the crocheted piece, so the feet are on the RS and the rest of the wire is on the surface of the WS. Sewing from the join at the top of the legs towards the foot, using the tail of yarn left after fastening off, sew the 41 stitches on each side of one leg together, encasing the wire. The last few stitches beyond the foot will form the hook. Repeat to finish the other leg. Make a bend, ⅝in (15mm) from each end of the covered wire. Make bends approximately 1⅝in (4cm) and 3⅛in (8cm) from each end, at the decreased sections of the crocheted legs. Make a bend in the centre, between the legs, and a bend where the covered wire emerges from the crocheted piece at each end, to finish the shaping. Sew in place near the top of the thorax, using A. Stitch all around the tops of the legs and through them, sewing over the wire inside the legs to attach them securely to the body.

Middle legs

Use pliers to bend approximately ¼in (6mm) into a loop at each end of the wire. Starting at the centre of the wire, wind yarn A tightly around the wire, starting at the foot and working over the end of the yarn to the middle. Wind a second layer in the opposite direction back over the wrapped wire to within 2⅛in (5.5cm) from the end. Wind a third layer back to the centre. Take the yarn to the end of the other leg and repeat to cover the other side in the same way. Trim the excess yarn and secure the end of the yarn with a dab of all-purpose adhesive and allow to dry.

Lay the covered wire down the centre of the length of the WS of one crocheted hind leg piece. Using the tail of yarn left after fastening off, sew the 16 stitches on each side of the crocheted leg together, encasing the middle of the wire. Make bends in the covered wire, ⅝in (1.5cm) and 2⅛in (5.5cm) from each end. Make a bend in the centre and at each end of the crocheted piece to finish shaping the legs. Sew to the base of the abdomen, near the thorax edging, using A. Sew around and through the crocheted tops of the legs, and over the wire inside, to attach them securely.

Hind legs

Bend each end of wire, as for the other legs, and wrap in A. Wind A tightly around the wire, starting at the foot and working over the end of the yarn to the middle. Wind a second layer in the opposite direction back over the wrapped wire to within 2⅜in (6cm) from the end. Wind a third layer back to the centre. Take the yarn to the end of the other leg and repeat to cover the other side in the same way. Trim yarn and secure with a dab of glue. Lay the covered wire down the centre of the length of the WS of the remaining crocheted hind leg piece and finish as for the middle legs. Make bends in the covered wire, ¾in (2cm) and 2⅜in (6cm) from each end. Make a bend in the centre and at each end of the crocheted piece to finish shaping the legs. Sew to the base of the abdomen, behind the middle legs, using A. Sew through and around the crocheted tops of the legs, as for the other legs, to attach them securely.

Wings

Trim the excess wire on the wings to within ⅛in (3mm). Use pliers to bend under the sharp ends. Pull the wing gently so the bent ends of the wire disappear just inside the stitches.

Position the wings behind the edging of the thorax and overlap them towards the wing tips. Sew the wings to the surface of the abdomen.

Weave in all the yarn ends.

Christmas beetle

The Christmas beetle is made using cotton and metallic threads held together to produce sparkly, jewel-like pieces. The threads come in an array of shades, so you can make a grand collection of colourful gems.

Materials

Light green and pink beetle
- DMC Coton Perlé 8, 100% cotton (87yd/80m per 10g ball):
  1 x 10g ball in 906 (A)
  1 x 10g ball in 224 (B)
  1 x 10g ball in 920 (C)
- DMC Diamant metallic thread, 72% viscose, 28% polyester (38yd/35m per reel):
  1 x reel in D3852 (D)
  1 x reel in D225 (E)
  1 x reel in D310 (F)

Gold and silver beetle
- DMC Coton Perlé 8:
  1 x 10g ball in 676 (A)
  1 x 10g ball in 3743 (B)
  1 x 10g ball in 402 (C)
- DMC Diamant metallic thread:
  1 x reel in D3821 (D)
  1 x reel in D415 (E)

Dark green and peach beetle
- DMC Coton Perlé 8:
  1 x 10g ball in 943 (A)
  1 x 10g ball in 402 (B)
  1 x 10g ball in 920 (C)

- DMC Diamant metallic thread:
  1 x reel in D699 (D)
  1 x reel in D301 (E)

All beetles
- 1.50mm (UK2½:US7) crochet hook
- Sharp-ended darning needle
- Small amount of toy stuffing
- 3 lengths of 26-gauge (0.4mm) craft wire, each measuring 5½in (14cm), for the legs
- 3⅛in (8cm) length of 26-gauge (0.4mm) craft wire for the antennae
- Clear nylon invisible thread
- 1 pair of ⁵⁄₃₂in (4mm) looped glass teddy bear eyes or beads
- Long-nose pliers
- All-purpose adhesive

Size
Approximately 2in (5cm) long, excluding antennae and legs.

Tension
40 sts and 40 rows to 4in (10cm) over double crochet using 1.50mm hook with A and D held together. Use larger or smaller hook if necessary to obtain correct tension.

Method

The Christmas beetle's body – the abdomen, pronotum (part of the thorax) and head – is crocheted in one piece, in continuous rounds and rows of double crochet. A line of stitches crocheted into unworked loops of a previous round forms an edging at the front and back of the pronotum. The wing cases are worked in rows of double crochet and joined to unworked loops of a previous round on the body by crocheting into each stitch of both pieces at the same time. The legs and antennae are made of craft wire wrapped in thread and bent into shape. The middle of the antennae is placed inside the front of the head and the edges are sewn together over the covered wire. The optional markings are embroidered with short stitches. The Christmas beetle is finished with glass eyes or beads.

1 ch at beg of the row/round does not count as a st throughout.

Body

Abdomen

With 1.50mm hook and A and D held tog, make a magic loop (see page 127).
Round 1: 1 ch, 6 dc into loop (6 sts).
Round 2 (inc): (Dc2inc) 6 times (12 sts).
Round 3 (inc): (Dc2inc, 1 dc) 6 times (18 sts).
Rounds 4–5: 1 dc in each dc.
Round 6 (inc): (Dc2inc, 2 dc) 6 times (24 sts).
Rounds 7–13: 1 dc in each dc.
Round 14 (dec): (Dc2tog, 2 dc) 6 times (18 sts).
Round 15: 1 dc in back loop only of next 12 dc, 1 dc in both loops of next 6 dc.

ABDOMEN

ROUNDS 1-15

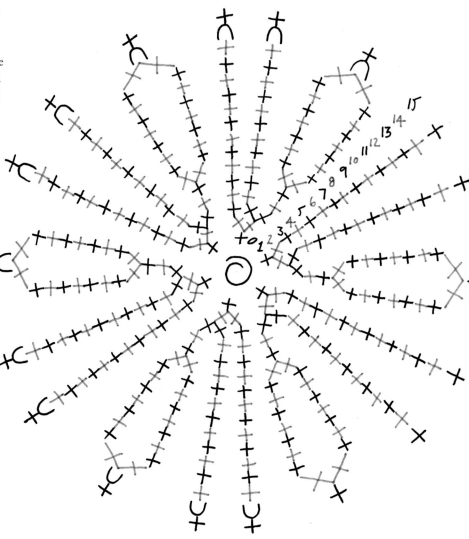

Pronotum

The following is worked in rows.
Row 1 (RS): 1 dc in each dc, turn.
Row 2 (WS): 1 ch, 1 dc in next
6 dc, 1 dc in front loop only of next
12 dc, turn.
Rows 3–4: 1 ch, 1 dc in each
dc, turn.

Head

Row 5 (dec): 1 ch, (dc2tog) in back
loops only 6 times, 1 dc in both loops
of next 6 dc, turn (12 sts).
Row 6 (dec): 1 ch, (dc2tog, 2 dc,
dc2tog) twice, sl st to first dc, turn
(8 sts).
Row 7: 1 ch, 1 dc in next 4 dc,
turn, finishing 4 sts before the end.
Row 8: 1 ch, 1 dc in next 4 dc.
Fasten off, leaving a long tail of
both threads.

PRONOTUM, HEAD

PRONOTUM: ROWS 1-4
HEAD: ROWS 5-8

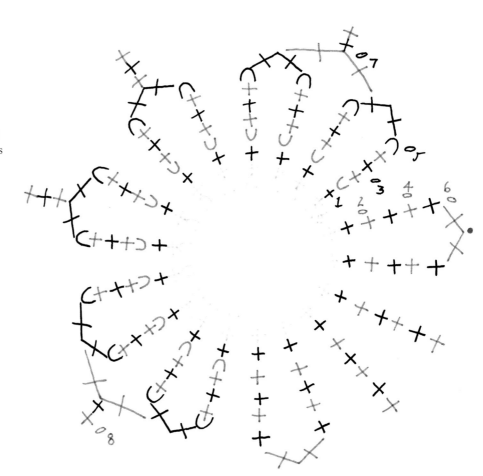

Key

⌒	Magic loop	✕⫟✕	dc3inc
⌀	Chain (ch)	✕✕	dc2tog
•	Slip stitch (sl st)	∩	work into back loop only
+	Double crochet (dc)	∪	work into front loop only
✕✕	dc2inc		

Pronotum edging

Front

Next: With head facing downwards, 1.50mm hook and A and D held tog, sl st in each of 12 unworked front loops of row 4 of pronotum. Fasten off, leaving a long tail of both threads.

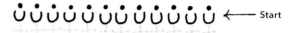

PRONOTUM EDGING

FRONT

Back

Next: With head facing upwards, 1.50mm hook and A and D held tog, sl st in first of 12 unworked back loops of row 1 of pronotum, 1 dc in same st as sl st, 1 dc in next 11 sts. Fasten off, leaving a long tail of both threads.

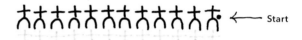

PRONOTUM EDGING

BACK

Elytra

(wing cases) (make 2)

With 1.50mm hook and B and E head tog, make 9 ch.

Row 1 (WS): 1 dc in 2nd ch from hook, 1 dc in next 6 ch, 3 dc in end ch, 1 dc in reverse side of next 7 ch, turn (17 sts).

Row 2 (RS) (inc): 1 ch, 1 dc in next 8 dc, dc3inc, 1 dc in next 8 dc, turn (19 sts).

Row 3 (inc): 1 ch, 1 dc in next 9 dc, dc3inc, 1 dc in next 9 dc, turn (21 sts).

Row 4 (inc): 1 ch, 1 dc in next 10 dc, dc3inc, 1 dc in next 10 dc (23 sts). Fasten off.

Do not fasten off the second elytra.

Next (RS): Rotate the elytra and work 6 dc evenly along edge of rows, with RS of remaining elytra facing, work 6 dc evenly along the edge to join.

Do not fasten off.

ELYTRA

ROWS 1-4

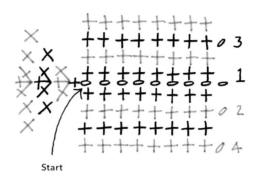

Start

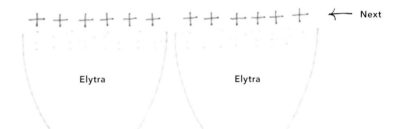

← Next

Elytra   Elytra

Join elytra to body

Next: With head facing downwards and tips of elytra pointing up, place WS of elytra on RS of body, aligning the 12 sts at the edge with the 12 unworked front loops of round 14 of abdomen. Inserting hook into each st of unworked loops of abdomen first, and then the corresponding st of the elytra, work 1 dc in next 12 sts at same time to join.

Fasten off, leaving a long tail of threads.

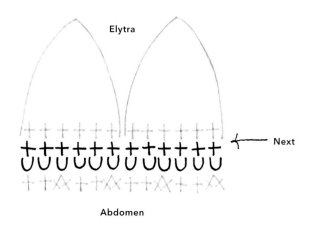

JOIN ELYTRA TO BODY

Making up

Body

Stuff the body, keeping the base flat. Sew together the open edges at the side of the pronotum. Use a tail of yarn left after joining the elytra to the body to sew them to the surface of the abdomen. Sew the corners of the edging on the front and back of the pronotum to the abdomen, using the tails of thread left after fastening off. Use F to embroider optional markings on the elytra with one or two short straight stitches for each (see page 133).

Antennae

Follow instructions to make the antennae on page 135, wrapping the wire in C. Place the finished antennae inside the opening at the top of the head. Sew together the four stitches of row 8 to the four unworked stitches of row 6, encasing the middle of the antennae. Bend the antennae into shape.

Legs

Follow instructions for the antennae on page 135 to make three pairs of legs. Wind C around the twisted wire, starting at the looped end of one leg and working over the end of the thread to the middle. Wind a second layer in the opposite direction back over the wrapped wire to within ⅜in (1cm) from the end. Wind a third layer back to the centre. Take the thread to the end of the other leg and repeat to cover the other side in the same way. Bend the legs to shape and sew them to the base of the body using C.

Eyes

Attach the glass eyes or beads using invisible nylon thread (see page 135).

Weave in all the thread ends.

Swallowtail butterflies

The combination of the 2-ply yarn and a variety of stitches and colour produces a delicately detailed butterfly. Specific stitching gives a subtle pattern to the wings.

Materials

- Scheepjes Maxi Sweet Treat, 100% cotton (153yd/140m per 25g ball):

Tiger swallowtail

1 x 25g ball in 280 Lemon (A)
1 x 25g ball in 110 Black (B)
2 lengths of 215 Royal Blue (C), each measuring approximately 33½in (85cm)
2 lengths of 722 Red (D), each measuring approximately 12in (30cm)

Zebra swallowtail

1 x 25g ball in 106 Snow White (A)
1 x 25g ball in 110 Black (B)
Approximately 20in (50cm) lengths of 722 Red (C) and 215 Royal Blue (D) for each hindwing
Approximately 12in (30cm) length of 722 Red (C) for antennae

Pipevine swallowtail

1 x 25g ball in 124 Ultramarine (A)
1 x 25g ball in 106 Snow White (B)
1 x 25g ball in 400 Petrol Blue (C)

All butterflies

- 1.25mm (UK3:US8) crochet hook
- Sharp-ended darning needle
- Small amount of toy stuffing
- 4 lengths of 26-gauge (0.4mm) craft wire, each measuring 8in (20cm), for the wings
- 3½in (9cm) length of 26-gauge (0.4mm) craft wire for the antennae
- Long-nose pliers
- All-purpose adhesive
- PVA glue

Size

Approximately 4in (10cm) wide and 3¼in (8.5cm) long.

Tension

42 sts and 44 rows to 4in (10cm) over half treble using 1.25mm hook. Use larger or smaller hook if necessary to obtain correct tension.

Method

The wings are made separately and worked in rows using a combination of stitches and colours to create the shape and pattern. The first row creates the 'cell' of the wing and the subsequent rows form the 'veins'.

The veins are crocheted in short rows. Only the front or back loop of each stitch of the cell is crocheted, to produce a subtle line around its edges. The markings on the wings are produced by working the first part of the stitch in a contrast colour and finishing the stitch with the main edging colour. The edging of the wings is crocheted around wire to give the wings structure. The body is worked in rows of double crochet. The edges are sewn together. The head, thorax and abdomen are defined by threading the yarn through the body between each section and winding it tightly around the underside. The eyes and other details on the head are embroidered. The antennae are made of craft wire wrapped in yarn and bent into shape. The pieces are sewn together. The tails of the wings are set with a thin coat of glue to finish the butterfly.

1 ch and 2 ch at beg of the row do not count as a st throughout.

Pattern note

Right forewing

Complete as for left forewing, working into front loop only, instead of back loop, where applicable. Odd rows are RS and even rows are WS. Edging is commenced on the WS.

Right hindwing

Complete as for left hindwing, working into front loop only, instead of back loop and back loop only, instead of front loop, where applicable. On the upper part of right hindwing, odd rows are WS and even rows are RS. On the lower part of right hindwing, odd rows are RS and even rows are WS. Edging is commenced on the WS of right hindwing.

COLOUR KEY

 A

 B

 C

 D

Tiger swallowtail

Left forewing

With 1.25mm hook and A, make 14 ch.
Row 1 (WS): 1 dc in 2nd ch from hook, 1 dc in next ch, 1 htr in next 2 ch, join B in last htr and carry unused yarn along the line of sts (see page 131), 1 tr in next 2 ch with B, 1 tr in next 2 ch with A, 1 tr in next 2 ch with B, 1 htr in next 2 ch with A, 4 dc in end ch with B, turn (16 sts).
Row 2 (RS): With A make 8 ch, 1 dc in 2nd ch from hook, 1 dc in next 2 ch, 1 dc in next 2 ch with B, 1 dc in next 2 ch with A, sl st in back loop only of last dc of row 1, turn. Continue on the 7 dc just worked.
Row 3: Dc2inc, 1 dc in next dc, with B work 1 dc in next 2 dc, with A work 1 dc in next dc, skip next dc, 1 dc in next dc, turn.
Row 4: 1 ch, 1 dc in next dc, skip next dc, 1 dc in next 5 dc, sl st in back loop only of next dc of row 1, turn (6 sts).
Row 5: 1 dc in next 4 dc, skip next dc, 1 dc in next dc, turn (5 sts).
Row 6: 1 ch, 1 dc in next dc, skip next dc, 1 dc in next 3 dc, 1 dc in back loop only of next dc of row 1, sl st in back loop only of next dc of row 1, turn.

Row 7: Dc2inc, 1 dc in next 2 dc, skip next dc, 1 dc in next dc, turn.
Row 8: 1 ch, 1 dc in next 5 dc, 1 dc in back loop only of next 2 htr of row 1, sl st in back loop only of next tr of row 1, turn (7 sts).
Row 9: 1 dc in next 5 dc, skip next dc, 1 dc in next dc, turn (6 sts).
Row 10: 1 ch, 1 dc in next 6 dc, 1 dc in back loop only of next 2 tr of row 1, sl st in back loop only of next tr of row 1, turn (8 sts).
Row 11: 1 dc in next 6 dc, skip next dc, 1 dc in next dc, turn (7 sts).

Row 12: 1 ch, 1 dc in next 7 dc; working in back loops only of row 1, 1 dc in next tr with B, with A work 1 dc in next tr, sl st in back loop only of next htr, turn (9 sts).
Row 13: 1 dc in next dc, 1 dc in next dc with B, with A work 1 dc in next 5 dc, skip next dc, 1 dc in next dc, turn (8 sts).
Row 14: 1 ch, 1 dc in next 6 dc, with B work 1 dc in next dc, with A work 1 dc in next dc; working in back loops only of row 1, 1 dc in next 3 sts, with B work 2 dc in same dc as last st, do not turn (13 sts).

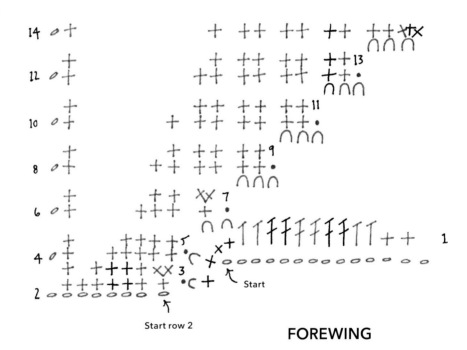

Start row 2

FOREWING

ROWS 1-14

Key

⌀ Chain (ch)

• Slip stitch (sl st)

✛ Double crochet (dc)

XX dc2inc

X✛X dc3inc

⊤ Half treble (htr)

⋁ htr2inc

Ŧ Treble (tr)

∩ work into back loop only on left wing
work into front loop only on right wing

∪ work into front loop only on left wing
work into back loop only on right wing

⊍ 2-htr puff

⊎ 3-htr puff

⊕ cluster

63

Forewing edging

Row 1 (RS): Rotate wing and, working around the craft wire with B and carrying yarn A along the line of stitches, work 1 dc in reverse side of next 13 ch of row 1 of wing, 1 dc in edge of last dc of row 1, 1 dc in reverse side of next 7 ch of row 2 of wing; leave wire and yarn A at tip of wing and carry them up on the WS of the edge of the next row, work 3 dc in same dc as last st, work 12 dc evenly down the edge of the rows, turn.
Row 2 (WS): 1 ch, 1 dc in next 15 dc, turn.
Row 3: Working around the craft wire and carrying unused yarn along the line of stitches, 1 ch, (1 dc in next dc with B, insert hook into next dc, yoh with yarn A and draw back through st, yoh with yarn B and draw through both loops to finish dc, 2 ch with B) 7 times, dc2inc; rotate wing and work 1 dc in edge of st on first row of edging, 1 dc in next 6 dc of row 14 with A, 1 dc in next dc with B, 1 dc in next 4 dc with A, 1 dc in next dc with B, dc2inc, sl st to next st. Fasten off, leaving a long tail of A and B.

FOREWING EDGING

ROWS 1-3

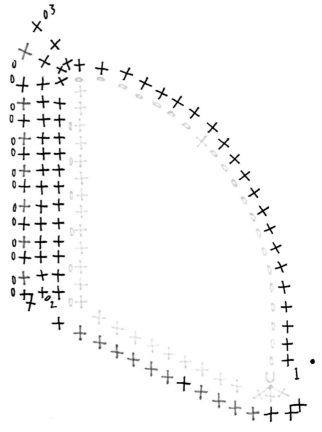

Left hindwing

Upper part

With 1.25mm hook and A, make 8 ch.

Row 1 (RS): 1 dc in 2nd ch from hook, 1 dc in next ch, 1 htr in next ch, 1 tr in next 2 ch, join B in last tr and carry unused yarn along the line of sts, 1 htr in next ch with B, with A work 2 dc in end ch, turn (8 sts).

Row 2 (WS): 3 ch with A, 1 dc in 2nd ch from hook, 1 dc in next ch, sl st in front loop only of last dc of row 1, turn.

Continue on the 2 dc just worked.

Row 3: Dc2inc, 1 dc in next dc, turn.

Row 4: 1 ch, 1 dc in next 3 dc; working in front loops only of row 1, 1 dc in next st with A, 1 dc in next st with B, sl st in next st, turn (5 sts).

Row 5: 1 dc in next dc with B, dc2inc with A, 1 dc in next dc, skip next dc, 1 dc in next dc, turn.

Row 6: 1 ch, 1 dc in next 4 dc, with B work 1 dc in next dc; working in front loops only of row 1, 1 dc in next 3 sts with A, dc3inc, do not turn.

Lower part

Row 1 (WS): Rotate wing and, working in reverse side of each ch of row 1 of upper part, 1 dc in next 6 ch with A, 1 dc in next ch with B, 1 dc in same st as last dc with A, 1 dc in reverse side of next 2 ch of row 2, turn (10 sts).

Row 2 (RS): 1 ch, 1 dc in next 2 dc, sl st in back loop only of next st of row 1, turn.

Continue on the 2 dc just worked.

Row 3: 1 dc in next 2 dc, turn.

Row 4: 1 ch, 1 dc in next dc with A, 1 dc in next dc with B, 1 dc in back loop only of next 2 dc of row 1 with A, sl st in back loop only of next dc, turn (4 sts).

Row 5: 1 dc in next 4 dc with A, turn.

HINDWING UPPER PART

ROWS 1-6

Start row 2

Start

HINDWING LOWER PART

ROWS 1-5

Hindwing edging

Row 1 (RS): Working around the craft wire with B and carrying yarn A along the line of stitches, work 1 ch, 1 dc in next 4 dc, 1 dc in back loop only of next 4 dc of row 1, 3 dc in next st of row 6 of upper part, with A work 1 dc in next 5 dc, with B work 1 dc in next dc, with A work 1 dc in next 4 dc, leave wire and yarn A at tip of wing and carry them up on the WS of the edge of the following rows; rotate wing, with B work 2 dc in same st as last dc, work 10 dc evenly down the edge of the rows, 1 dc in same st as last st, turn.

Row 2 (WS): 1 ch, 1 dc in next dc, *yoh with yarn C, insert hook into next dc, yoh and draw back through st, yoh, insert hook into same st, yoh and draw back through st, yoh with yarn B and draw through all 5 loops to finish 2-htr puff stitch*, **1 htr in next dc with B, yoh with yarn C, insert hook into next dc, yoh and draw back through st, yoh and draw through 2 loops on hook, (yoh with C, insert hook in same st, yoh and draw back through st, yoh and draw through 2 loops on hook) twice, yoh with yarn B and draw through all 4 loops to finish cluster stitch; rep from ** 3 more times, 1 htr in next dc with B; rep from * to *, 1 dc in next dc with B, turn.

Row 3: Skip first st, 1 dc in next 6 sts, (1 htr in next st, htr2inc) twice, make cluster st with D and finish st with B, 1 dc in next dc with B, turn.

Row 4: 1 ch, 1 dc in next 14 sts, turn.

Row 5: Working around the craft wire and carrying unused yarn along the line of stitches, skip first dc, ***1 dc in next st with B, yoh with yarn A, insert hook into next dc, yoh and draw back through st, (yoh with yarn A, insert hook in same st, yoh and draw back through st) twice, yoh with yarn B and draw through all 7 loops to finish 3-htr puff stitch, 3 ch; rep from *** 3 more times, leave wire and yarn A at last st, make 4 ch, sl st in 2nd ch from hook, sl st in next 2 ch, 1 dc in next 2 ch to shape the tail of the wing, skip next ch; working around the craft wire and carrying unused yarn along the line of stitches, rep from *** twice more, 4 dc in next dc, work 3 dc evenly down edge of previous 3 rows, sl st in first dc of row 1 of edging. Fasten off.

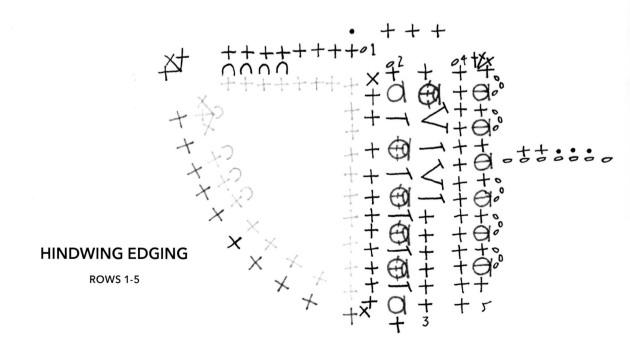

HINDWING EDGING

ROWS 1-5

Body

With 1.25mm hook and B, make 12 ch.

Row 1 (RS): 1 dc in 2nd ch from hook, 1 dc in next 9 ch, 2 dc in end ch, 1 dc in reverse side of next 10 ch. Join A in last dc, turn (22 sts).

Row 2 (WS): With A, 1 ch, 1 dc in next 10 dc, (dc2inc) twice, 1 dc in next 10 dc, turn (24 sts).

Row 3: 1 ch, 1 dc in next 11 dc, (dc2inc) twice, 1 dc in next 11 dc, sl st to first dc, finishing at the head end (26 sts).

Fasten off, leaving a long tail of A and B.

BODY

ROWS 1-3

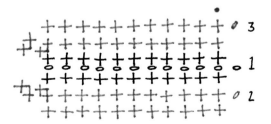

Zebra swallowtail

Left forewing

With 1.25mm hook and A, make 14 ch.
Rows 1–2: Work as for rows 1–2 of Tiger Swallowtail forewing, page 63.
Row 3: Dc2inc with A, 1 dc in next 3 dc with B, 1 dc in next dc with A, skip next dc, 1 dc in next dc, turn.
Row 4: 1 ch, 1 dc in next dc with A, skip next dc, 1 dc in next 3 dc with B, 1 dc in next 2 dc with A, sl st in back loop only of next dc of row 1, turn (6 sts).
Row 5: 1 dc in next 2 dc with A, 1 dc in next 2 dc with B, skip next dc, 1 dc in next dc, turn (5 sts).
Row 6: 1 ch, 1 dc in next dc with B, skip next dc, 1 dc in next dc, 1 dc in next 2 dc with A, 1 dc in back loop only of next dc of row 1, sl st in back loop only of next dc, turn.
Row 7: Dc2inc with A, 1 dc in next dc, 1 dc in next dc with B, skip next dc, 1 dc in next dc, turn.
Row 8: 1 ch, 1 dc in next 2 dc with B, 1 dc in next 3 dc with A, 1 dc in back loop only of next 2 htr of row 1, sl st in back loop only of next tr, turn (7 sts).
Row 9: 1 dc in next 5 dc with A, skip next dc, 1 dc in next dc with B, turn (6 sts).
Row 10: 1 ch, 1 dc in next dc with B, 1 dc in next 5 dc with A, 1 dc in back loop only of next 2 tr of row 1 with B, sl st in back loop only of next tr, turn (8 sts).
Row 11: 1 dc in next 2 dc with B, 1 dc in next 4 dc with A, skip next dc, 1 dc in next dc, turn (7 sts).
Row 12: 1 ch, 1 dc in next 5 dc with A, 1 dc in next 2 dc with B, 1 dc in back loop only of next 2 tr of row 1, sl st in back loop only of next htr, turn (9 sts).
Row 13: 1 dc in next 4 dc with B, 1 dc in next 3 dc with A, skip next dc, 1 dc in next dc, turn (8 sts).
Row 14: 1 ch, 1 dc in next 4 dc with A, 1 dc in next 3 dc with B, 1 dc in next dc with A; working in back loops only of row 1, 1 dc in next 3 sts, with B work 2 dc in same st as last st, do not turn (13 sts).

FOREWING

ROWS 1-14

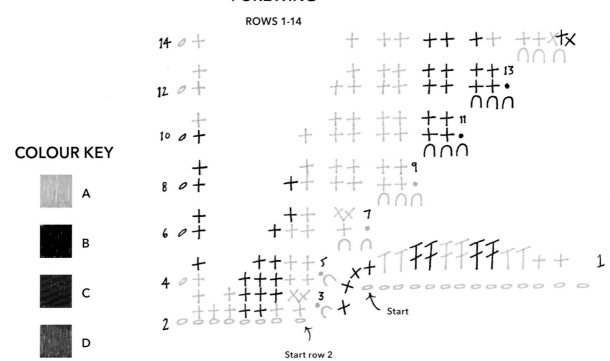

COLOUR KEY

A

B

C

D

Start

Start row 2

Forewing edging

Rows 1–2: Work as for rows 1–2 of Tiger Swallowtail forewing edging (see page 64).

Row 3: Working around the craft wire and carrying unused yarn along the line of stitches, 1 ch, (1 dc in next dc with B, insert hook into next dc, yoh with yarn A and draw back through st, yoh with yarn B and draw through both loops to finish dc, 2 ch with B) 7 times, dc2inc; rotate wing and work 1 dc in edge of st on first row of edging, 1 dc in next 6 dc with A, 1 dc in next dc with B, 1 dc in next 4 dc with A, 1 dc in next dc with B, dc2inc, sl st to next st.

Fasten off, leaving a long tail of A and B.

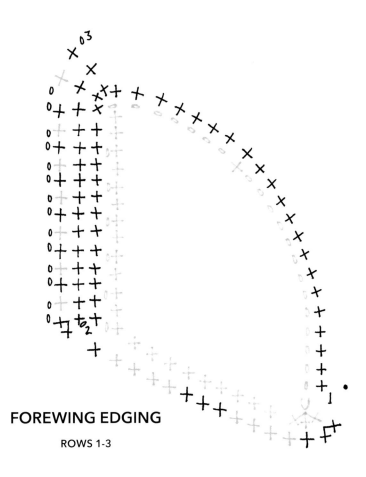

FOREWING EDGING

ROWS 1-3

Left hindwing

Upper part

With 1.25mm hook and A, make 8 ch.

Row 1 (RS): 1 dc in 2nd ch from hook, 1 dc in next ch, 1 htr in next ch, 1 tr in next 2 ch, join B in last tr and carry unused yarn along the line of sts, 1 htr in next ch with B, 1 dc in next ch, with A work 1 dc in same ch as last st, turn (8 sts).

Rows 2–3: As for Tiger Swallowtail, page 65.

Row 4: 1 ch, 1 dc in next 3 dc, with B work 1 dc in front loop only of next 2 sts of row 1, sl st in front loop only of next st, turn (5 sts).

Row 5: 1 dc in next 2 dc with B, 1 dc in same st as last dc with A, 1 dc in next dc, skip next dc, 1 dc in next dc, turn.

Row 6: 1 ch, 1 dc in next 3 dc with A, 1 dc in next 2 dc with B; working in front loops only of row 1 with A, 1 dc in next 3 sts, dc3inc, do not turn.

Lower part

Row 1 (WS): Rotate wing and work 1 dc in reverse side of next 6 ch of row 1 of upper part with A, 2 dc in reverse side of next ch with B, 1 dc in reverse side of next 2 ch of row 2 with A, turn (10 sts).

Rows 2–5: As for Tiger Swallowtail (see page 65).

HINDWING UPPER PART

ROWS 1-6

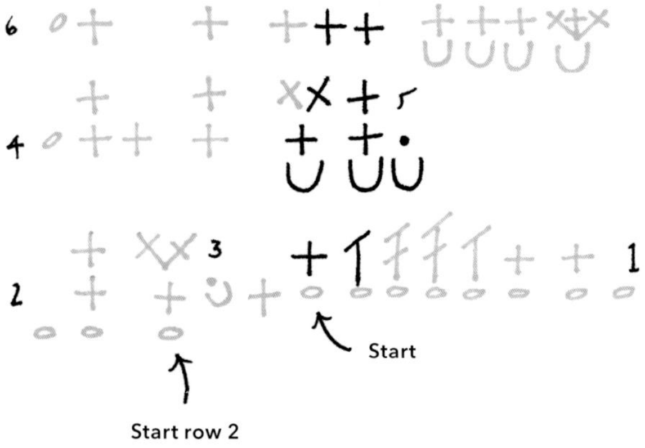

HINDWING LOWER PART

ROWS 1-5

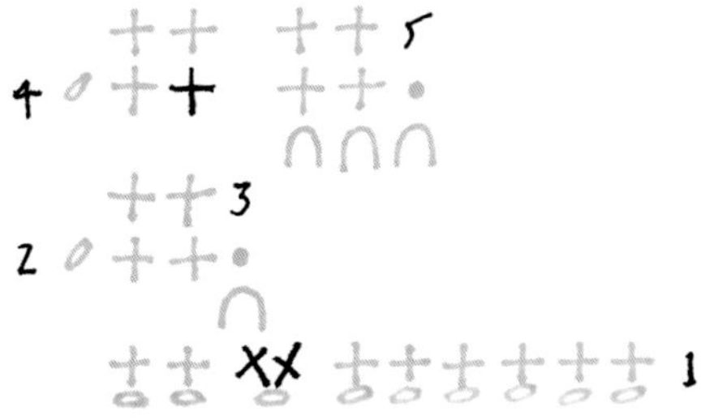

Hindwing edging

Row 1 (RS): Working around the craft wire with B and carrying yarn A along the line of stitches, work 1 ch, 1 dc in next 4 dc, 1 dc in back loop only of next 4 dc of row 1, 3 dc in next st of row 6 of upper part, with A work 1 dc in next 5 dc, 1 dc in next 2 dc with B, 1 dc in next 3 dc with A; leave wire at tip of wing and carry it up on the WS of the edge of the following rows; rotate wing and work 2 dc in same st as last dc, work 10 dc evenly down the edge of the rows, changing to yarn B for the last 2 sts, 1 dc in same st as last st with B, turn.

Row 2 (WS): 1 ch, 1 dc in next dc with B, *yoh with yarn C, insert hook into next dc, yoh and draw back through st, yoh and draw through 2 loops on hook, (yoh with C, insert hook in same st, yoh and draw back through st, yoh and draw through 2 loops on hook) twice, yoh with yarn B and draw through all 4 loops to finish cluster stitch*, 1 htr in next 5 dc, 1 dc in next 6 dc, turn.

Row 3: Skip first st, 1 dc in next 6 sts with B, 1 htr in next st, htr2inc; rep from * to *, with A work htr2inc, 1 htr in next st, 1 dc in next dc, turn.

Row 4: With B, 1 ch, 1 dc in next 14 sts, turn.

Row 5: Working around the craft wire and carrying unused yarn along the line of stitches, skip first dc, ***1 dc in next st with B, yoh with yarn A, insert hook into next dc, yoh and draw back through st, (yoh with yarn A, insert hook in same st, yoh and draw back through st) twice, yoh with yarn B and draw through all 7 loops to finish 3-htr puff stitch, 3 ch***; rep from *** to *** 3 more times, leave wire and yarn A at last st, make 6 ch, sl st in 2nd ch from hook, sl st in next 2 ch, 1 dc in next 4 ch to shape the tail of the wing, skip next ch; working around the craft wire and carrying unused yarn along the line of stitches, rep from *** to *** twice more using D instead of A, dc2inc, work 3 dc evenly down edge of previous 3 rows, sl st in first dc of row 1 of edging.
Fasten off.

Body

Work as for Tiger Swallowtail (see page 67).

HINDWING EDGING

ROWS 1-5

BODY

ROWS 1-3

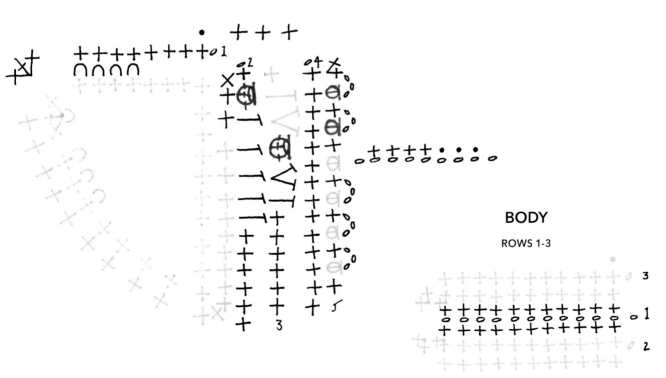

Pipevine swallowtail

Left forewing

Follow chart for Tiger Swallowtail (see page 63), working with A throughout.

With 1.25mm hook and A, make 14 ch.

Row 1 (WS): 1 dc in 2nd ch from hook, 1 dc in next ch, 1 htr in next 2 ch, 1 tr in next 6 ch, 1 htr in next 2 ch, 4 dc in end ch, turn (16 sts).

Row 2 (RS): 8 ch, 1 dc in 2nd ch from hook, 1 dc in next 6 ch, sl st in back loop only of last dc of row 1, turn.

Continue on the 7 dc just worked.

Row 3: Dc2inc, 1 dc in next 4 dc, skip next dc, 1 dc in next dc, turn.

Rows 4–11: Work as for rows 4–11 of Tiger Swallowtail forewing, page 63.

Row 12: 1 ch, 1 dc in next 7 dc, 1 dc in back loop only of next 2 tr of row 1, sl st in back loop only of next htr of row 1, turn (9 sts).

Row 13: 1 dc in next 7 dc, skip next dc, 1 dc in next dc, turn (8 sts).

Row 14: 1 ch, 1 dc in next 8 dc; working in back loops only of row 1, 1 dc in next 2 sts, 3 dc in next st, do not turn (13 sts).

COLOUR KEY

 A

 B

 C

FOREWING EDGING
ROWS 1-3

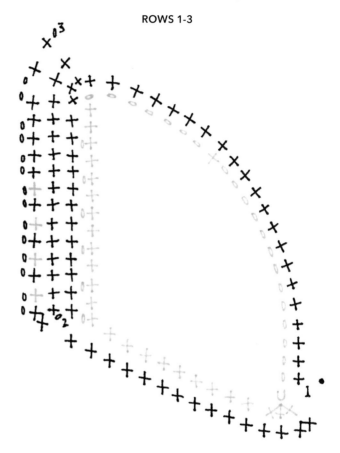

Forewing edging

Row 1 (RS): Rotate wing and, working around the craft wire, 1 dc in reverse side of next 13 ch of row 1 of wing, 1 dc in edge of last dc of row 1, 1 dc in reverse side of next 7 ch of row 2 of wing; leave wire at tip of wing and carry it up on the WS of the edge of the next row, work 3 dc in same dc as last st, work 12 dc evenly down the edge of the rows, turn.

Row 2 (WS): 1 ch, 1 dc in next 15 dc, turn.

Row 3: Working around the craft wire and, carrying unused yarn along the line of stitches, 1 ch, (1 dc in next 2 dc, 2 ch) 3 times, (1 dc in next dc with A, insert hook into next dc, yoh with yarn B and draw back through st, yoh with A and draw through both loops to finish dc, 2 ch with A) 4 times, dc2inc; rotate wing, with A work 1 dc in edge of st on first row of edging, 1 dc in next 12 dc, dc2inc, sl st to next st.

Fasten off, leaving a long tail of yarn A.

Left hindwing

Upper part

Follow chart for Tiger Swallowtail hindwing (see page 65), working with C throughout.

With 1.25mm hook and C, make 8 ch.

Row 1 (RS): 1 dc in 2nd ch from hook, 1 dc in next ch, 1 htr in next ch, 1 tr in next 2 ch, 1 htr in next ch, 2 dc in end ch, turn (8 sts).

Rows 2–3: As for Tiger Swallowtail hindwing (see page 65).

Row 4: 1 ch, 1 dc in next 3 dc, 1 dc in front loop only of next 2 sts of row 1, sl st in front loop only of next st, turn (5 sts).

Row 5: 1 dc in next dc, dc2inc, 1 dc in next dc, skip next dc, 1 dc in next dc, turn.

Row 6: 1 ch, 1 dc in next 5 dc; working in front loops only of row 1, 1 dc in next 3 sts, dc3inc, do not turn.

Lower part

Follow chart for Tiger Swallowtail hindwing (see page 65), working with C throughout.

Row 1 (WS): Rotate wing and work 1 dc in reverse side of next 6 ch of row 1 of upper part, 2 dc in reverse side of next ch, 1 dc in reverse side of next 2 ch of row 2, turn (10 sts).

Rows 2–3: As for Tiger Swallowtail, page 65.

Row 4: 1 ch, 1 dc in next 2 dc, 1 dc in back loop only of next 2 dc of row 1, sl st in back loop only of next dc, turn (4 sts).

Row 5: 1 dc in next 4 dc, turn.

Hindwing edging

Row 1 (RS): Working around the craft wire, 1 ch, 1 dc in next 4 dc, 1 dc in back loop only of next 4 dc of row 1, 3 dc in next st of row 6 of upper part, 1 dc in next 10 dc, leave wire at tip of wing and carry it up on the WS of the edge of the following rows; rotate wing and work 2 dc in same st as last dc, work 10 dc evenly down the edge of the rows, 1 dc in same st as last st, turn.

Row 2 (WS): 1 ch, 1 dc in next dc, (1 htr in next dc, htr2inc) twice, 1 htr in next dc, 1 dc in next 7 dc, turn.

Row 3: Skip first st, ***1 dc in next st with C, yoh with yarn B, insert hook into next st, yoh and draw back through st, (yoh with yarn B, insert hook in same st, yoh and draw back through st) twice, yoh with yarn C

and draw through all 7 loops to finish 3-htr puff stitch; rep from *** 5 more times, 1 dc in next 2 sts with C, turn.

Row 4: 1 ch, 1 dc in next dc, 1 htr in next 12 sts, 1 dc in next dc, turn.

Row 5: Working around the craft wire, skip first dc, (1 dc in next 2 sts with C, 3 ch with B) 3 times, 1 dc in next st with C, leave wire at last st, make 7 ch, sl st in 2nd ch from hook, sl st in next 2 ch, 1 dc in next 2 ch to shape the tail of the wing, skip next ch; working around the craft wire and carrying unused yarn along the line of stitches, 1 dc in next st with C, (3 ch with B, 1 dc in next 2 sts with C) twice, 4 dc in next dc, work 3 dc evenly down edge of previous 3 rows, sl st in first dc of row 1 of edging. Fasten off.

Body

With 1.25mm hook and A, make 12 ch.

Row 1 (RS): 1 dc in 2nd ch from hook, 1 dc in next 5 ch, join C in last dc and work 1 dc in next 4 dc, 2 dc in end ch, 1 dc in reverse side of next 4 ch, with A work 1 dc in reverse side of next 6 ch, turn (22 sts).

Row 2 (WS): 1 ch, 1 dc in next 6 dc, with C work 1 dc in next 4 dc, (dc2inc) twice, 1 dc in next 4 dc, with A work 1 dc in next 6 dc, turn (24 sts).

Row 3: 1 ch, 1 dc in next 6 dc, with C work 1 dc in next 5 dc, (dc2inc) twice, 1 dc in next 5 dc, with A work 1 dc in next 6 dc, sl st to first dc, finishing at the head end (26 sts). Fasten off, leaving a long tail of A and C.

HINDWING EDGING

ROWS 1-5

BODY

ROWS 1-3

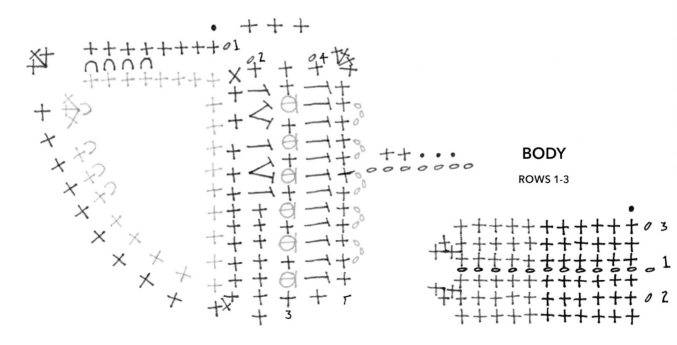

Making up

Body

With A, sew together the opening at the front of the head. Sew together the 16 stitches on each side of the body with whip stitch (see page 132) using matching yarn and stuffing the body before sewing the last few stitches. With B, or C for the Pipevine, embroider six or seven stitches close together on each side of the head for the eyes. With A, insert the needle just behind an eye, between a stitch on row 1, through the body and out through other side, between the corresponding stitch, keeping the yarn on the underside of the body. Pull tightly on the yarn to shape the head. Work two more stitches over the first, pulling tightly on the yarn. Using C for the Pipevine, and A for the Tiger and Zebra Swallowtails, work three stitches over each other in the same way as before, halfway down the body, to define the thorax and abdomen. On the Tiger and Zebra Swallowtails, embroider two straight stitches next to each other with B, over the front of the head, between the eyes. Embroider six tiny short stitches with B on top of the Pipevine Swallowtail's head.

Antennae

Follow the instructions to make and attach the antennae on page 135, wrapping the antennae in yarn A for the Pipevine, B for the Tiger and C for the Zebra Swallowtail. Wind the yarn around the twisted wire, starting at the tip of one antenna and working over the end of the yarn to the middle. Take the yarn to the tip of the other antenna and wrap it evenly and tightly back along the length, finishing at the middle. Trim the excess yarn. Secure the end of the yarn with a dab of all-purpose adhesive and allow to dry. Use yarn to match the butterfly's head to sew a few stitches through the top of the head and over the centre of the covered wire to attach the antennae.

Wings

Trim the excess wire on the wings to within ⅛in (3mm). Use pliers to bend under the sharp ends. Pull the wing gently so the bent ends of the wire disappear just inside the stitches. Use the tail of yarn left after fastening off to sew the edges of the forewing and hindwing together where they will be joined to the body. Sew a few stitches where the wings overlap, approximately ⅝in (1.5cm) from the joined edges.

Sew the wings to each side of the thorax between the head and the abdomen, stitching neatly along the top and underside of the wings to attach them securely in place. Apply a thin coat of PVA glue to the WS of the tail of the hindwings. Lay the butterfly on its back and stick a pin through each end of the tail to hold it in shape while it dries.

Weave in all the yarn ends.

Dragonfly

The delicate looking wings of the dragonfly are
created by using metallic embroidery thread, together
with an openwork pattern and various stitch lengths.

Materials

- Anchor Freccia, 100% cotton (311yd/285m
  per 50g ball):
  1 x 50g ball in 01442 (A)
  1 x 50g ball in 00255 (B)
  1 x 50g ball in 00632 (C)
- Metallic stranded embroidery thread, such as
  DMC Light Effects, shade E135, for the wings
- 1.75mm (UK2:US6) crochet hook
- Sharp-ended darning needle
- Small amount of toy stuffing
- 6¼in (16cm) length of 18-gauge (1mm) craft wire
  for the body
- 4 lengths of 26-gauge (0.4mm) craft wire,
  each measuring 11in (28cm), for the wings
- 3 lengths of 26-gauge (0.4mm) craft wire,
  each measuring 7in (18cm), for the legs
- Long-nose pliers
- All-purpose adhesive

Size

Approximately 4½in (11.5cm) long, excluding legs.

Tension

34 sts and 33 rows to 4in (10cm) over double
crochet using 1.75mm hook. Use larger or smaller
hook if necessary to obtain correct tension.

Method

The dragonfly's abdomen and thorax are crocheted in one piece, in rows of double crochet. The first row of the thorax is worked along the edge of the rows of the abdomen. The head is worked in rounds and the eyes are shaped by crocheting various stitches, plus increasing and decreasing. The wings are crocheted with metallic stranded embroidery thread using a variety of stitches to create a curved shape and an open pattern. The last round is crocheted around wire. The wings are stitched to the top of the thorax. The legs are made of craft wire wrapped in crochet thread and bent into shape after sewing them to the underside of the thorax. Wire is inserted into the narrow abdomen to keep its shape. The thorax and head are stuffed and sewn together. Embroidery finishes the abdomen and eyes.

1 ch at beg of the row/round does not count as a st throughout.

Body

Abdomen

With 1.75mm hook and A,
make 21 ch.
Row 1 (WS): 1 dc in 2nd ch from hook, 1 dc in each ch to end, 1 dc in reverse side of each ch, turn (40 sts).
Row 2 (RS): 1 ch, 1 dc in each dc to end. Do not turn.
Do not fasten off.

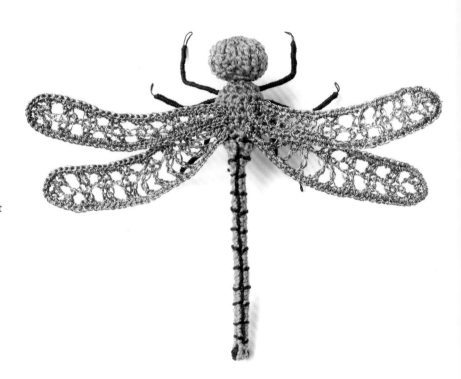

ABDOMEN

ROWS 1-2

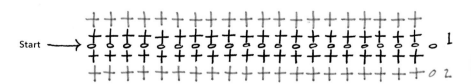

78

Thorax

Row 1 (RS): Rotate abdomen and work 3 dc evenly along edge of rows, turn (3 sts).

Row 2 (WS) (inc): 1 ch, dc2inc, 1 dc in next dc, dc2inc, turn (5 sts).

Row 3: 1 ch, 1 dc in each dc to end, turn.

Row 4 (inc): 1 ch, (dc2inc) 5 times, join B in last dc, turn (10 sts). Continue with B.

Row 5: 1 ch, 1 dc in each dc to end, turn.

Row 6 (inc): 1 ch, (dc2inc, 1 dc) 5 times, turn (15 sts).

Rows 7–8: 1 ch, 1 dc in each dc to end, turn.

Row 9 (dec): 1 ch, (dc2tog, 1 dc) 5 times, turn (10 sts).

Row 10: 1 ch, 1 dc in each dc to end. Fasten off, leaving a long tail of A and B.

THORAX

ROWS 1-10

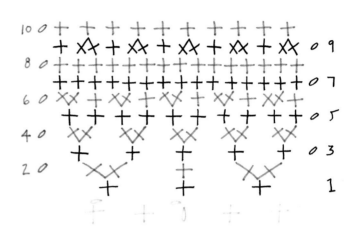

Key

⟲ Magic loop

⟋ Chain (ch)

• Slip stitch (sl st)

+ Double crochet (dc)

✕✕ dc2inc

✕✕✕ dc3inc

⋏⋏ dc2tog

⊤ Half treble (htr)

𝖥 Treble (tr)

⋁𝖥 tr2inc

𝖥 Double treble (dtr)

79

Head

With 1.75mm hook and B, make a magic loop (see page 127).
Round 1: 1 ch, 6 dc into loop (6 sts).
Round 2 (inc): (Dc2inc) 6 times. Join A in last dc and carry unused thread on WS of work (12 sts). Pull tightly on short end of thread to close loop.

Eyes

Round 3 (inc): With A, *(1 dc, 1 htr) in next dc, (tr2inc) twice, (1 htr, 1 dc) in next dc; rep from *; with B work 1 dc in next 4 dc (20 sts).
Round 4 (dec): With A, *1 dc in next dc, 1 htr in next htr, 1 tr in next 4 tr, 1 htr in next htr, 1 dc in next dc; rep from *; with B, (dc2tog) twice (18 sts).

Finish head

Continue with B.
Round 5 (dec): (Dc2tog) 8 times, 1 dc in next 2 dc (10 sts).
Round 6: 1 dc in each dc.
Fasten off, leaving a long tail of B.

HEAD

ROUNDS 1-2

EYES, FINISH HEAD

EYES: ROUNDS 3-4
FINISH HEAD: ROUNDS 5-6

Forewings (make 2)

With 1.75mm hook and two strands of embroidery thread, make 30 ch.
Round 1: *1 dc in 2nd ch from hook, 1 dc in next ch, (2 ch, skip 2 ch, 1 dc in next 2 ch) twice, (2 ch, skip 2 ch, 1 htr in next 2 ch) 4 times, 2 ch, skip 2 ch to finish top of wing, (1 htr, 2 ch, 3 htr, 2 ch, 1 htr) in end ch*; working in reverse side of each ch, (2 ch, skip 2 ch, 1 htr in next 2 ch) twice, (2 ch, skip 2 ch, 1 htr in next ch, 2 ch, 1 htr in next ch) twice, (2 ch, skip 2 ch, 1 dc in next 2 ch) 3 times to finish lower part of wing (33 sts and 18 2-ch sps).
Do not fasten off.

Forewing edging

Round 2: Working around the craft wire, *2 dc in next dc, 1 dc in next dc, (2 dc in next 2-ch sp, 1 dc in next 2 dc) twice, (2 dc in next 2-ch sp, 1 dc in next 2 htr) 4 times, (2 dc in next 2-ch sp, 1 dc in next htr) twice, dc3inc (1 dc in next htr, 2 dc in next 2-ch sp) twice*, (1 dc in next 2 htr, 2 dc in next 2-ch sp) twice, (1 dc in next htr, 2 dc in next 2-ch sp) 4 times, (1 dc in next 2 dc, 2 dc in next 2-ch sp) twice, 1 dc in next dc, 2 dc in next dc, sl st to first st (73 sts).
Fasten off, leaving a long tail of thread.

FOREWING, FOREWING EDGING

FOREWINGS: ROUND 1
FOREWING EDGING: ROUND 2

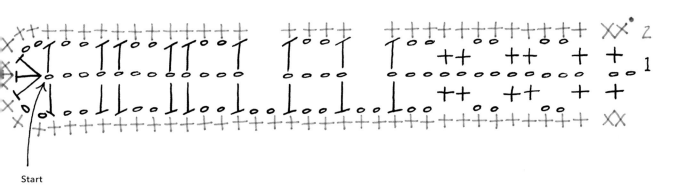

Start

Hindwings (make 2)

With 1.75mm hook and two strands of embroidery thread, make 30 ch.

Round 1: Rep from * to * of round 1 of forewing; working in reverse side of each ch, 2 ch, skip 2 ch, 1 htr in next 2 ch, (2 ch, skip 2 ch, 1 tr in next 2 ch) twice, (2 ch, skip 2 ch, 1 dtr in next ch, 2 ch, 1 dtr in next ch) twice, 2 ch, skip 2 ch, 1 dtr in next ch, 1 tr in next ch, 2 ch, skip 2 ch, 1 htr in next ch, 1 dc in next ch to finish lower part of wing (33 sts and 18 2-ch sps).
Do not fasten off.

Hindwing edging

Round 2: Working around the craft wire, rep from * to * of round 2 of forewing; continuing around the craft wire, 1 dc in next 2 htr, 2 dc in next 2-ch sp, (1 dc in next 2 tr, 2 dc in next 2-ch sp) twice, (1 dc in next dtr, 2 dc in next 2-ch sp) 4 times, 1 dc in next dtr, 1 dc in next tr, 2 dc in next 2-ch sp, 1 dc in next htr, 2 dc in next dc, sl st to first st (73 sts).
Fasten off, leaving a long tail of thread.

HINDWING, HINDWING EDGING

HINDWINGS: ROUND 1
HINDWING EDGING: ROUND 2

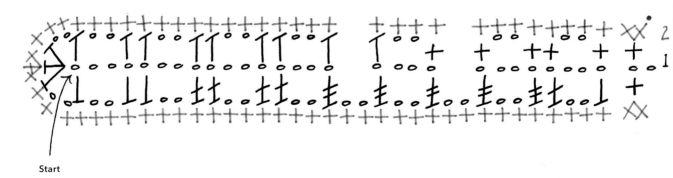

Start

82

Making up

Body

Use pliers to bend approximately ¼in (6mm) into a loop at each end of the wire and squeeze together. Bend the wire in the centre so the looped ends are together. Thread the tail of thread through the last row of the thorax and pull up tightly to close. Sew together the edges of the thorax. Stuff the thorax. Sew together the 20 stitches on each side of the abdomen with whip stitch (see page 132) with tail of thread left after fastening off, inserting the wire into the body, so the looped ends are just inside the stuffed thorax, before sewing the last few stitches together. Using C, embroider vertical and horizontal stitches down the length of the abdomen. Embroider the two appendages at the end of the abdomen in satin stitch (see page 133) with C.

Head

Stuff the head. Thread a tail of B through the last round, pulling tightly on the end to close the opening. Sew to the end of the thorax. Embroider a single straight stitch (see page 133) between the eyes at the top of the head with B. Embroider one or two glints of light in each eye in satin stitch using two strands of embroidery thread used for the wings.

Legs

Follow instructions for the antennae on page 135 to make three pairs of legs. Wind C around the twisted wire, working over the thread end, to the centre. Take the thread across to the opposite end and wind tightly around wire, back to the centre. Trim the

excess thread and secure the end of the thread with a dab of all-purpose adhesive and allow to dry. Bend the legs to shape and sew them to the base of the body with C.

Wings

Trim the excess wire on the wings to within ⅛in (3mm). Use pliers to bend under the sharp ends. Pull the wing gently so the bent ends of the wire disappear just inside the stitches. Flip one forewing and hindwing so

the wings mirror each other. Sew the wings to the thorax, stitching neatly around the tops to attach them securely.

Weave in all the thread ends.

Ladybird

This seven-spot ladybird's markings are embroidered.
Other species of ladybird can be made following the same
pattern, but changing the colour and number of spots.

Materials

- Rico Essentials Crochet,
  100% cotton (306yd/280m per 50g ball):
  1 x 50g ball in 012 Black (A)
  1 x 50g ball in 004 Red (B)
  1 x 50g ball in 001 White (C)
- 1.75mm (UK2:US6) crochet hook
- Sharp-ended darning needle
- Small amount of toy stuffing
- 3 lengths of 26-gauge (0.4mm) craft wire,
  each measuring 4¾in (12cm), for the legs
- 1⅝in (4cm) length of 26-gauge (0.4mm) craft wire
  for the antennae
- Stranded embroidery thread in black
- Clear nylon invisible thread
- 1 pair of ⁵⁄₃₂in (4mm) looped glass teddy bear eyes
  or beads
- Long-nose pliers
- All-purpose adhesive

Size

Approximately 1⅜in (3.5cm) long,
excluding antennae and legs.

Tension

38 sts and 38 rows to 4in (10cm) over double
crochet using 1.75mm hook. Use larger or smaller
hook if necessary to obtain correct tension.

Method

The ladybird's head, pronotum (part of thorax) and abdomen are crocheted in one piece, in continuous rounds of double crochet. A line of stitches crocheted into unworked loops of a previous round forms an edge over the top of the pronotum. The wing cases are worked in rows of double crochet and joined to unworked loops of a previous round on the body by crocheting into each stitch of both pieces at the same time. The spots and other markings are embroidered. The legs are made of craft wire wrapped in yarn and bent into shape. The antennae are made in the same way and wrapped in embroidery thread so they are finer than the legs. The ladybird is finished with glass eyes or beads.

1 ch at beg of the row/round does not count as a st throughout.

Body

Head

With 1.75mm hook and A, make a magic loop (see page 127).
Round 1: 1 ch, 6 dc into loop (6 sts).
Round 2 (inc): (Dc2inc) 6 times (12 sts).
Pull tightly on short end of yarn to close loop.

HEAD

ROUNDS 1-2

Pronotum

Round 3: 1 dc in back loop only of each dc.

Round 4 (inc): (Dc2inc) 6 times, 1 dc in next 6 dc (18 sts).

Round 5: 1 dc in back loop only of next 12 dc, 1 dc in both loops of next 6 dc.

Round 6: 1 dc in each dc.

PRONOTUM

ROUNDS 3-6

Key

- ⟳ Magic loop
- ⟋ Chain (ch)
- • Slip stitch (sl st)
- ┼ Double crochet (dc)
- ⋊⋉ dc2inc
- ⋊┼⋉ dc3inc
- ⋊⋉ dc2tog
- ⋂ work into back loop only
- ⋃ work into front loop only

87

Abdomen

Round 7 (inc): (Dc2inc, 2 dc) 4 times in back loops only, (dc2inc, 2 dc) twice in both loops (24 sts).

Rounds 8–11: 1 dc in each dc.

Round 12 (dec): (Dc2tog, 2 dc) 6 times (18 sts).

Rounds 13–14: 1 dc in each dc.

Round 15 (dec): (Dc2tog, 1 dc) 6 times (12 sts).

Rounds 16–17: 1 dc in each dc. Fasten off, leaving a long tail of yarn.

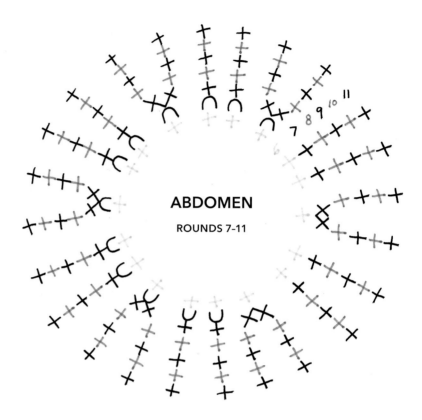

ABDOMEN

ROUNDS 7-11

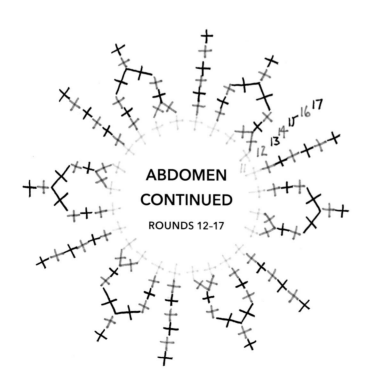

ABDOMEN CONTINUED

ROUNDS 12-17

Pronotum edging

Next: With head facing upwards, 1.75mm hook and A, sl st in first of 12 unworked front loops of round 4 of pronotum, behind the head; beg in same st as sl st, 1 dc in next 12 sts. Fasten off, leaving a long tail of yarn.

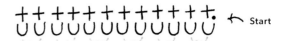

**PRONOTUM
EDGING**

Elytra
(wing cases) (make 2)

With 1.75mm hook and B, make 8 ch.
Row 1 (WS): 1 dc in 2nd ch from hook, 1 dc in next 5 ch, 3 dc in end ch, 1 dc in reverse side of next 6 ch, turn (15 sts).
Row 2 (RS) (inc): 1 ch, 1 dc in next 7 dc, dc3inc, 1 dc in next 7 dc, turn (17 sts).
Row 3 (inc): 1 ch, 1 dc in next 8 dc, dc3inc, 1 dc in next 8 dc, turn (19 sts).
Row 4 (inc): 1 ch, 1 dc in next 9 dc, dc3inc, 1 dc in next 9 dc (21 sts).
Fasten off.
Do not fasten off the second elytra.
Next (RS): Rotate the elytra and work 6 dc evenly along edge of rows, with RS of remaining elytra facing, work 6 dc evenly along the edge to join.
Do not fasten off.

Join elytra to body

Next: With head facing downwards and tips of elytra pointing up, place WS of elytra on RS of body, aligning the 12 sts at the edge with the 12 unworked front loops of round 6 of pronotum. Inserting hook into each st of unworked loops of pronotum first, and then the corresponding st of the elytra, work 1 dc in next 12 sts at same time to join.
Fasten off, leaving a long tail of yarn.

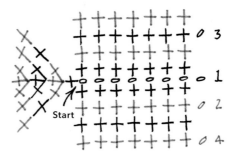

ELYTRA

ROWS 1-4

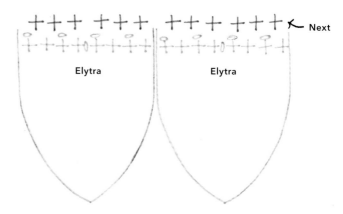

ELYTRA CONTINUED

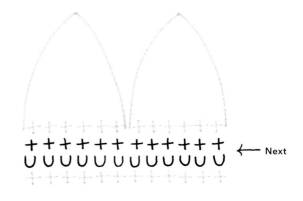

JOIN ELYTRA TO BODY

Making up

Body

Stuff the body, keeping the base flat. Thread the tail of yarn through the last round of the body and pull up tightly to close. Use the tail of yarn left after joining the elytra to the body to sew them to the surface of the abdomen. Use the tail of yarn to sew each corner of the pronotum edging to the abdomen. Embroider the spots and other markings in satin stitch (see page 133) with A and C.

Antennae

Follow instructions to make and attach the antennae as seen on page 135, wrapping the wire in two strands of black embroidery thread. Sew to the head using two strands of embroidery thread.

Legs

Follow instructions for the antennae on page 135 to make three pairs of legs, wrapping the wire with A. Make two bends on each side of the covered wire to shape the legs and sew to the base of the body using A.

Eyes

Attach the glass eyes or beads using invisible nylon thread (see page 135).

Weave in all the yarn ends.

Mirror spider

Metallic embroidery thread is used to sew
a scattering of reflective sequins over the abdomen
of this mirror spider to catch the light.

Materials

- ◆ Rico Essentials Crochet, 100% cotton
  (306yd/280m per 50g ball):
  1 x 25g ball in 025 Gold (A)
  1 x 25g ball in 002 Beige (B)
- ◆ Metallic stranded embroidery thread,
  such as DMC Light Effects, shade E168
- ◆ 1.75mm (UK2:US6) crochet hook
- ◆ Sharp-ended darning needle
- ◆ Small amount of toy stuffing
- ◆ 4 lengths of 18-gauge (1mm) craft wire,
  each measuring 6¾in (17cm), for the legs
- ◆ 3in (7.5cm) length of 26-gauge (0.4mm) craft wire
  for the palps
- ◆ Approximately 80 x ³⁄₁₆in (5mm) square sequins in a
  metallic colour, such as Silver Iris
- ◆ 8 size 11/0, ¹⁄₁₆in (2mm) black seed beads
- ◆ Stranded embroidery thread in black
- ◆ Clear nylon invisible thread
- ◆ Long-nose pliers
- ◆ All-purpose adhesive

Size

Approximately 4in (10cm) long, including legs.

Tension

38 sts and 38 rows to 4in (10cm) over double
crochet using 1.75mm hook. Use larger or smaller
hook if necessary to obtain correct tension.

Method

The mirror spider's abdomen and cephalothorax are crocheted separately in continuous rounds of double crochet. The legs and palps are made with craft wire wrapped in yarn, sewn to the body and bent into shape. Beads are sewn to the front of the spider for the eyes. Sequins are sewn over the abdomen using metallic thread. The spider is finished with an embroidered fly stitch behind its eyes.

Abdomen

With 1.75mm hook and A, make a magic loop (see page 127).
Round 1: 1 ch (does not count as st), 6 dc into loop (6 sts).
Round 2 (inc): (Dc2inc, 1 dc) 3 times (9 sts).
Pull tightly on short end of yarn to close loop.
Round 3: 1 dc in each dc.

ABDOMEN

ROUNDS 1-20

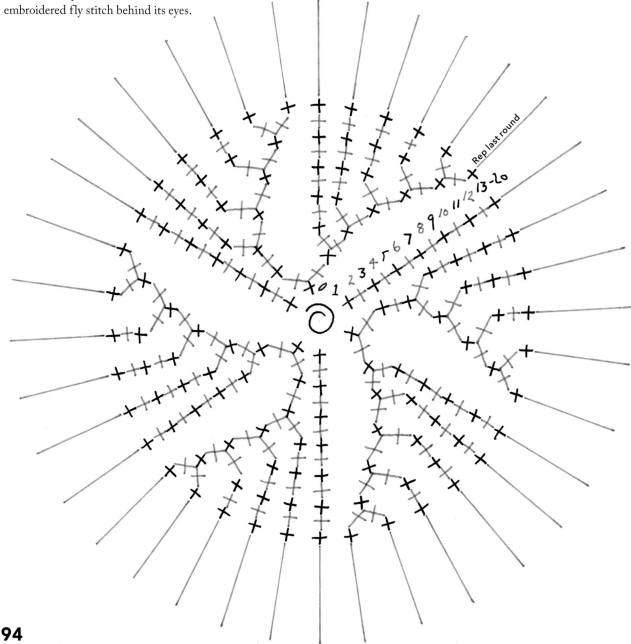

Round 4 (inc): (Dc2inc, 2 dc)
3 times (12 sts).
Round 5: 1 dc in each dc.
Round 6 (inc): (Dc2inc, 1 dc)
6 times (18 sts).
Round 7: 1 dc in each dc.
Round 8 (inc): (Dc2inc, 2 dc)
6 times (24 sts).
Round 9: 1 dc in each dc.
Round 10 (inc): (Dc2inc, 3 dc)
6 times (30 sts).
Round 11: 1 dc in each dc.

Round 12 (inc): (Dc2inc, 4 dc)
6 times (36 sts).
Rounds 13–20: 1 dc in each dc.
Round 21 (dec): (Dc2tog, 4 dc)
6 times (30 sts).
Round 22 (dec): (Dc2tog, 3 dc)
6 times (24 sts).
Round 23 (dec): (Dc2tog, 2 dc)
6 times (18 sts).
Round 24 (dec): (Dc2tog, 1 dc)
6 times (12 sts).
Fasten off, leaving a long tail of yarn.

ABDOMEN
CONTINUED
ROUNDS 21-24

Key

○   Magic loop

𝒐   Chain (ch)

•   Slip stitch (sl st)

✛   Double crochet (dc)

✕✕   dc2inc

✕✕   dc2tog

Cephalothorax
(thorax and head)

With 1.75mm hook and B,
make a magic loop.
Round 1: 1 ch (does not count as st),
5 dc into loop (5 sts).
Round 2 (inc): (Dc2inc) 5 times
(10 sts).
Round 3: 1 dc in each dc.
Round 4 (inc): (Dc2inc, 1 dc)
5 times (15 sts).
Rounds 5–9: 1 dc in each dc.
Round 10 (dec): (Dc2tog, 1 dc)
5 times (10 sts).
Fasten off, leaving a long tail of yarn.

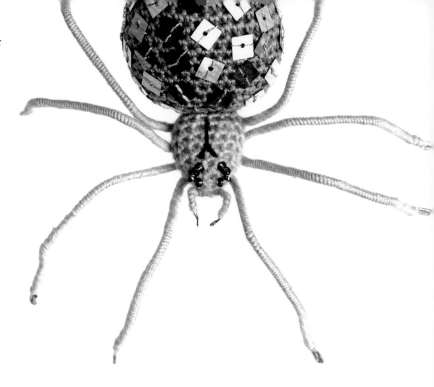

CEPHALOTHORAX

ROUNDS 1-10

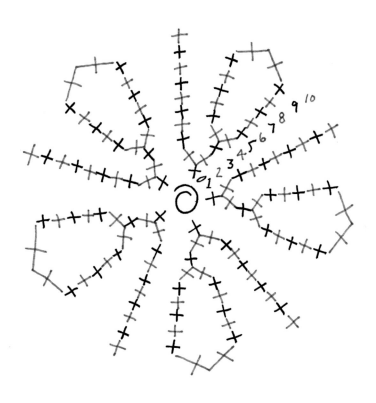

Making up

Cephalothorax

Stuff the cephalothorax. Thread the tail of crochet thread through the last round and pull up tightly to close. Sew the seed beads to the cephalothorax for the eyes using invisible thread (see page 135).

Legs

Use pliers to bend back approximately ¼in (6mm) from each end of the wire and squeeze together. Wind B tightly around the wire, working over the yarn end, to the centre. Take the thread across to the opposite end and wind tightly around wire, back to the centre. Trim the excess thread and secure the end of the yarn with a dab of all-purpose adhesive and allow to dry. Sew to the base of the cephalothorax using B. Bend legs to shape.

Palps

Follow the instructions for the antennae on page 135 to make the palps, wrapping the wire with B. Sew to the front of the cephalothorax using B.

Abdomen

Stuff the abdomen. Thread a tail of yarn through the last round and pull up tightly to close. Sew the abdomen to the cephalothorax. Sew sequins over the surface of the abdomen using one strand of metallic embroidery thread. Finish the spider with embroidered fly stitch (see page 134) on top of the cephalothorax, using two strands of black embroidery thread.

Weave in all the yarn ends.

Moths

The harnessed tiger moth uses colourwork and
puff stitches to create the markings on the wings.
The leopard and white ermine moths' details are finished
with decorative embroidery. A combination of smooth
cotton and fluffy yarn is used for each moth.

Materials
- Scheepjes Maxi Sweet Treat, 100% cotton
  (153yd/140m per 25g ball):

Harnessed tiger moth
  1 x 25g ball in 110 Black (A)
  1 x 25g ball in 130 Old Lace (B)
  1 x 25g ball in 189 Royal Orange (C)

Leopard moth
  1 x 25g ball in 105 Bridal White (A)
  1 x 25g ball in 281 Tangerine (B)
  1 x 25g ball in 110 Black (C)
  1 x 25g ball in 400 Petrol Blue (E)

White ermine moth
  1 x 25g ball in 105 Bridal White (A)
  1 x 25g ball in 281 Tangerine (B)
  1 x 25g ball in 110 Black (C)

All moths
- Scheepjes Alpaca Rhythm, 80% alpaca,
  20% extra fine wool (219yd/200m per 25g ball):
  1 x 25g ball in 670 Bop (D)
- 1.25mm (UK3:US8) crochet hook
- Sharp-ended darning needle
- Small amount of toy stuffing
- 4 lengths of 26-gauge (0.4mm) craft wire,
  each measuring 10in (25cm), for the wings
- 3½in (9cm) length of 26-gauge (0.4mm) craft wire
  for the antennae
- Long-nose pliers
- All-purpose adhesive

Size
Approximately 4½in (11.5cm) wide and 2⅜in (6cm) long.

Tension
42 sts and 44 rows to 4in (10cm) over double
crochet using 1.25mm hook. Use larger or
smaller hook if necessary to obtain correct tension.

Method

The moths' wings, body and thorax are made separately. The tiger moth's wings are worked in rows using a combination of colourwork and stitches to create the markings. The edging of each wing is crocheted around wire to hold each wing's shape. The leopard and white ermine moths' wings are worked in one colour and in double crochet throughout. The details on their wings are embroidered before sewing the

finished pieces of the moth together. The abdomen is worked in rows of double crochet. The first row of the head is crocheted along the rows of the abdomen. The edges of the head and abdomen are sewn together and the body is stuffed. The eyes and details on the abdomen and thorax are embroidered. The antennae are made of craft wire wrapped in yarn and bent into shape.

1 ch and 2 ch at beg of the row do not count as a st throughout.

Pattern note

Right forewing

Complete as for left forewing. Odd rows are WS and even rows are RS. Edging is commenced on the WS.

Right hindwing

Complete as for left hindwing. On the upper part of left hindwing, odd rows are WS and even rows are RS. On the lower part of left hindwing, odd rows are RS and even rows are WS. Edging is commenced on the WS of right hindwing.

COLOUR KEY

 A

 B

C

FOREWINGS

ROWS 1-13

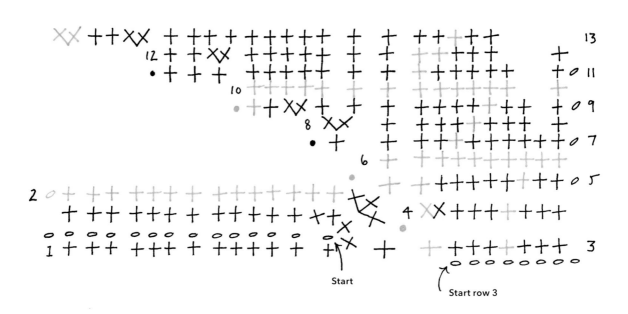

Start

Start row 3

Harnessed tiger moth

Left forewing

With 1.25mm hook and A, make 14 ch.
Row 1 (RS): 1 dc in 2nd ch from hook, 1 dc in next 11 ch, 5 dc in end ch, 1 dc in reverse side of next 12 ch, join B in last dc, turn (29 sts).
Carry unused yarn along line of sts.
Row 2 (WS): With B, 1 ch, 1 dc in next 14 dc, with A work 3 dc in next dc, 1 dc in next dc, turn, finishing 13 sts before end of row (31 sts).
Row 3: 8 ch, 1 dc in 2nd ch from hook, 1 dc in next 2 ch; 1 dc in next ch with B; 1 dc in next 3 ch with A, 1 dc in last dc of row 2 with B, sl st in next dc, turn.
Continue on the 8 dc just worked.
Row 4: 1 dc in first dc with B, dc in same st as last st with A, 1 dc in next 3 dc, with B work 1 dc in next dc, with A work 1 dc in next 3 dc, turn (9 sts).
Row 5: With A, 1 ch, 1 dc in next 2 dc; 1 dc in next dc with B, 1 dc in next 5 dc with A, 1 dc in next dc with B, 1 dc in next dc of row 2, sl st in next dc, turn (10 sts).
Row 6: With B, 1 dc in each dc to end, turn.
Row 7: With A, 1 ch, 1 dc in next 6 dc; 1 dc in next dc with B, 1 dc in next 3 dc with A, 1 dc in next dc of row 2, sl st in next dc, turn (11 sts).
Row 8: Dc2inc with A, 1 dc in next 4 dc; 1 dc in next dc with B, 1 dc in next 3 dc with A, skip next dc, 1 dc in next dc, turn.
Row 9: With A, 1 ch, 1 dc in next 3 dc; 1 dc in next dc with B, 1 dc in next 7 dc with A, 2 dc in next dc of row 2, 1 dc in next dc; with B, 1 dc in next dc, sl st in next dc, turn (15 sts).
Row 10: With B, 1 dc in next 13 dc, skip next dc, 1 dc in next dc, turn (14 sts).
Row 11: With A, 1 ch, 1 dc in next 6 dc; 1 dc in next dc with B, 1 dc in next 7 dc with A, 1 dc in next 3 dc of row 2, sl st in next dc, turn (17 sts).
Row 12: With A, 1 dc in next 2 dc, dc2inc, 1 dc in next 7 dc; 1 dc in next 2 dc with B, 1 dc in next 3 dc with A, skip next dc, 1 dc in next dc, turn.
Row 13: With A, skip first dc, 1 dc in next 2 dc; 1 dc in next dc with B, 1 dc in next 13 dc with A, 2 dc in next dc of row 2, 1 dc in next 2 dc; with B, 2 dc in next dc, do not turn (22 sts).

Forewing edging

Row 1 (RS): Rotate wing and, working around the craft wire with B, 2 dc in next dc of row 1 of wing, 1 dc in next 12 dc, 1 dc each in edge of rows 1 and 2, 1 dc in reverse side of next 6 ch of row 3 of wing, 2 dc in next ch, work 10 dc evenly down the edge of the rows, 2 dc in next dc of row 13, 1 dc in next 20 dc, dc2inc, sl st to first st (58 sts).
Fasten off, leaving a long tail of B.

Key

⟋   Chain (ch)

•   Slip stitch (sl st)

✝   Double crochet (dc)

✗✗   dc2inc

✗✝✗   dc3inc

◖◗   3-htr puff

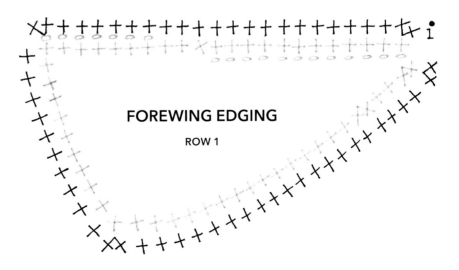

FOREWING EDGING

ROW 1

Left hindwing

Upper part

With 1.25mm hook and C, make 12 ch.

Row 1 (RS): 1 dc in 2nd ch from hook, 1 dc in next 9 ch, 2 dc in end ch, turn (12 sts).

Row 2 (WS): 7 ch, 1 dc in 2nd ch from hook, 1 dc in next 5 ch, 2 dc in last dc of row 1, 1 dc in next 2 dc, sl st in next dc, turn.

Continue on the 10 dc just worked.

Row 3: 1 dc in next 8 sts; carrying unused yarn across line of sts, *yoh with yarn A, insert hook into next dc, yoh and draw back through st, (yoh with yarn A, insert hook in same st, yoh and draw back through st) twice, yoh with yarn C and draw through all 7 loops to finish 3-htr puff stitch*; 1 dc in next dc with C, turn.

Row 4: 1 ch, 1 dc in next 3 sts with C; rep from * to *, 1 dc in next 6 dc with C, 2 dc in next dc of row 1, 1 dc in next 2 dc, sl st in next st, turn (13 sts and 1 3-htr puff st).

Row 5: 1 dc in next 12 sts; rep from * to *, 1 dc in next dc with C, turn.

Row 6: Skip first dc, 1 dc in next 13 sts, 2 dc in next dc of row 1, 1 dc in next 2 dc, dc2inc, do not turn (19 sts).

Lower part

Row 1 (WS): Rotate wing and, 1 dc in reverse side of next 11 ch of row 1 of upper part with C, 1 dc in edge of st of row 2, working in reverse side of each ch of row 2, 1 dc in next 2 ch; rep from * to * of row 3 of upper part, 1 dc in next 3 ch, turn (17 sts and 1 3-htr puff st).

Row 2 (RS): 1 ch, 1 dc in next 11 sts, sl st in next dc, turn.

Continue on the 11 dc just worked.

Row 3: 1 dc in next 8 dc; rep from * to *, skip next dc, 1 dc in next dc with C, turn (9 sts and 1 3-htr puff st).

Row 4: 1 ch, 1 dc in next 10 sts with C, 2 dc in next dc of row 2, 1 dc in next 2 dc, sl st in next dc, turn (14 sts).

Row 5: 1 dc in next 9 dc; rep from * to *, 1 dc in next 2 dc, skip next dc, 1 dc in next dc, turn (12 dc and 1 3-htr puff st).

Row 6: Skip first dc, 1 dc in next 12 sts, 2 dc in next dc of row 2, 1 dc in next dc, join B in last dc, do not turn (15 sts).

HINDWING, UPPER PART

ROWS 1-6

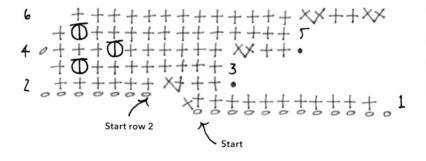

HINDWING, LOWER PART

ROWS 1-6

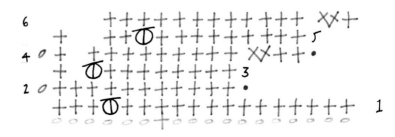

Hindwing edging

Row 1 (RS): Working around the craft wire with B and carrying yarn C along the line of stitches, 2 dc in next dc of row 6 of upper part, 1 dc in next 17 dc, dc2inc, work 10 dc evenly down edge of rows, 2 dc in next dc of row 6 of lower part; with C work 1 dc in next 13 dc, dc2inc, sl st to first st. Fasten off, leaving a long tail of B and C.

HINDWING EDGING

ROW 1

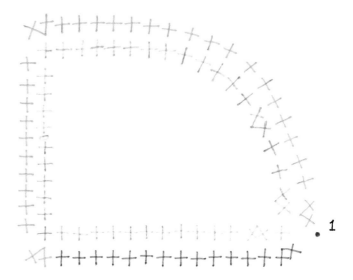

Body

Abdomen

With 1.25mm hook and C, make
18 ch.

Row 1 (RS): 1 dc in 2nd ch from
hook, 1 dc in next 15 ch, join A in last
dc and work 2 dc in end ch; with C
work 1 dc in reverse side of next 16 ch,
turn (34 sts).

Row 2 (WS) (inc): 1 ch, 1 dc in next
16 dc with C, (dc2inc) twice with A, 1
dc in next 16 dc with C, turn (36 sts).

Row 3 (inc): 1 ch, 1 dc in next 16 dc
with C, 1 dc in next dc with A,
(dc2inc) twice, 1 dc in next dc, with C
work 1 dc in next 16 dc, turn (38 sts).

Row 4 (inc): 1 ch, 1 dc in next 16 dc
with C, 1 dc in next 2 dc with A,
(dc2inc) twice, 1 dc in next 2 dc,
with C work 1 dc in next 16 dc, turn
(40 sts).

Row 5 (inc): 1 ch, 1 dc in next 16 dc
with C, 1 dc in next 3 dc with A,
(dc2inc) twice, 1 dc in next 3 dc, with
C work 1 dc in next 16 dc, join D in
last dc, do not turn (42 sts).
Do not fasten off.

ABDOMEN

ROWS 1-5

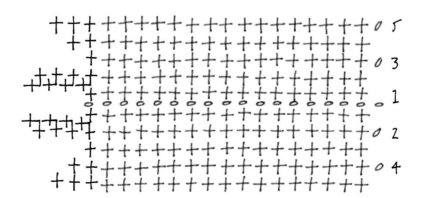

HEAD

ROWS 1-4

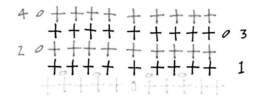

THORAX

ROWS 1-6

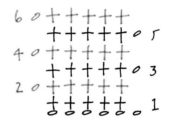

THORAX CONTINUED

Head

Row 1 (RS): Rotate abdomen and work 9 dc evenly along edge of rows with D, turn (9 sts).

Row 2 (WS): 1 ch, 1 dc in each dc to end, turn.

Rows 3–4: Rep row 2.

Fasten off, leaving a long tail of A and C and D.

Thorax

With 1.25mm hook and D doubled, make 6 ch.

Row 1 (RS): 1 dc in 2nd ch from hook, 1 dc in next 4 ch, turn (5 sts).

Row 2 (WS): 1 ch, 1 dc in each dc to end, turn.

Rows 3–6: Rep row 2. Do not turn at end of row 6.

Next (WS): Rotate the piece and work 5 dc evenly along edge of rows to finish top of thorax.

Fasten off, leaving a long tail of yarn.

Leopard moth

Left forewing

Follow chart for harnessed tiger moth (see page 100), working with A throughout. With 1.25mm hook and A, make 14 ch.

Row 1 (RS): 1 dc in 2nd ch from hook, 1 dc in next 11 ch, 5 dc in end ch, 1 dc in reverse side of next 12 ch, turn (29 sts).

Row 2 (WS): 1 ch, 1 dc in next 14 dc, dc3inc, 1 dc in next dc, turn, finishing 13 sts before end of row (31 sts).

Row 3: 8 ch, 1 dc in 2nd ch from hook, 1 dc in next 6 ch, 1 dc in last dc of row 2, sl st in next dc, turn. Continue on the 8 dc just worked.

Row 4: Dc2inc, 1 dc in each dc to end, turn (9 sts).

Row 5: 1 ch, 1 dc in next 9 dc, 1 dc in next dc of row 2, sl st in next dc, turn (10 sts).

Row 6: 1 dc in each dc to end, turn.

Row 7: 1 ch, 1 dc in next 10 dc, 1 dc in next dc of row 2, sl st in next dc, turn (11 sts).

Row 8: Dc2inc, 1 dc in next 8 dc, skip next dc, 1 dc in next dc, turn.

Row 9: 1 ch, 1 dc in next 11 dc, 2 dc in next dc of row 2, 1 dc in next 2 dc, sl st in next dc, turn (15 sts).

Row 10: 1 dc in next 13 dc, skip next dc, 1 dc in next dc, turn (14 sts).

Row 11: 1 ch, 1 dc in next 14 dc, 1 dc in next 3 dc of row 2, sl st in next dc, turn (17 sts).

Row 12: 1 dc in next 2 dc, dc2inc, 1 dc in next 12 dc, skip next dc, 1 dc in next dc, turn.

Row 13: Skip first dc, 1 dc in next 16 dc, 2 dc in next dc of row 2, 1 dc in next 2 dc, dc2inc, do not turn (22 sts).

Forewing edging

With A, work as for harnessed tiger moth forewing edging (see page 101). Fasten off, leaving a long tail of yarn.

Left hindwing

Upper part

With 1.25mm hook and A, make 12 ch.

Rows 1–2: Work as for rows 1–2 of harnessed tiger moth hindwing (see page 102).

Row 3: 1 dc in each dc to end, turn.

Row 4: 1 ch, 1 dc in next 10 dc, 2 dc in next dc of row 1, 1 dc in next 2 dc, sl st in next st, turn (14 sts).

Row 5: 1 dc in each dc to end, turn.

Row 6: Skip first dc, 1 dc in next 13 sts, 2 dc in next dc of row 1, 1 dc in next 2 dc, dc2inc, do not turn (19 sts).

Lower part

Row 1 (WS): Rotate wing and, 1 dc in reverse side of next 11 ch of row 1 of upper part, 1 dc in edge of st of row 2, working in reverse side of each ch of row 2, 1 dc in next 6 ch, turn (18 sts).

Row 2 (RS): 1 ch, 1 dc in next 11 sts, sl st in next dc, turn.

Continue on the 11 dc just worked.

Row 3: 1 dc in next 9 dc, skip next dc, 1 dc in next dc, turn (10 sts).

Row 4: 1 ch, 1 dc in next 10 sts, 2 dc in next dc of row 2, 1 dc in next 2 dc, sl st in next dc, turn (14 sts).

Row 5: 1 dc in next 12 dc, skip next dc, 1 dc in next dc, turn (13 sts).

Row 6: Skip first dc, 1 dc in next 12 sts, 2 dc in next dc of row 2, 1 dc in next dc, do not turn (15 sts).

Hindwing edging

Work as for harnessed tiger moth hindwing edging (see page 103), using A throughout.

Fasten off, leaving a long tail of yarn.

HINDWING, UPPER PART

ROWS 1-6

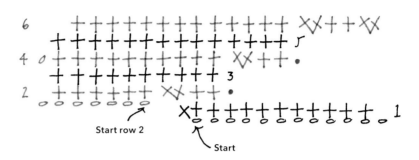

HINDWING, LOWER PART

ROWS 1-6

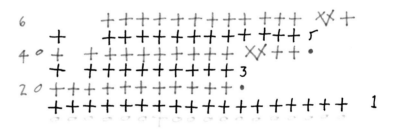

Body

Abdomen

Follow chart for harnessed tiger moth (see page 104), using B for rows 1–2 and A for rows 3–5.

With 1.25mm hook and B, make 18 ch.

Row 1 (RS): 1 dc in 2nd ch from hook, 1 dc in next 15 ch, 2 dc in end ch, 1 dc in reverse side of next 16 ch, turn (34 sts).

Row 2 (WS) (inc): 1 ch, 1 dc in next 16 dc, (dc2inc) twice, 1 dc in next 16 dc, join A in last dc, turn (36 sts). Continue with A.

Row 3 (inc): 1 ch, 1 dc in next 17 dc, (dc2inc) twice, 1 dc in next 17 dc, turn (38 sts).

Row 4 (inc): 1 ch, 1 dc in next 18 dc, (dc2inc) twice, 1 dc in next 18 dc, turn (40 sts).

Row 5 (inc): 1 ch, 1 dc in next 19 dc, (dc2inc) twice, 1 dc in next 19 dc, join D in last dc, do not turn (42 sts). Do not fasten off.

Head

Work as for harnessed tiger moth
(see page 105) with yarn D.
Fasten off, leaving a long tail of
A and D.

Thorax

Work as for harnessed tiger moth
(see page 105).

White ermine moth

Follow instructions as for leopard moth (see page 106) and charts for harnessed tiger moth (see page 100), working with A throughout.

Making up

Body

Thread the tail of D through the last round of the head, and pull up tightly to close. Sew together the edges of the head. Sew together the 21 stitches on each side of the abdomen with whip stitch (see page 132) using matching yarn and stuffing the body before sewing the last few stitches. Embroider six or seven stitches close together on each side of the head for the eyes, using A for the harnessed tiger moth and C for the leopard and white ermine moths.

Embroider horizontal lines of satin stitch (see page 133) down the back of the harnessed tiger moth's abdomen with A. With A doubled, embroider three lazy daisy stitches (see page 134) on the thorax and two short stitches above them. Sew the top of the thorax to the central stitches of the first row of the head.

Embroider horizontal and vertical lines of satin stitch down the centre of the leopard moth's back with E. Embroider horizontal lines of satin stitch around the sides of the abdomen. On the thorax, embroider satin stitch dots with E and circles with C by working four short stitches in a cross with a space in the centre, then weave the yarn once or twice through the stitches.

With C, embroider satin stitch down the centre and around the sides of the white ermine moth's abdomen. Embroider a line of short stitches beneath the line of satin stitches around the sides.

Antennae

Follow instructions to make and attach the antennae on page 135, wrapping the wire in yarn A for harnessed tiger moth and C for leopard and white ermine moths.

Wings

Trim the excess wire on the wings to within ⅛in (3mm). Use pliers to bend under the sharp ends. Pull each wing gently so the bent ends of the wire disappear just inside the stitches.

With C, embroider circles, as on the thorax, and satin stitch markings on the leopard moth forewings. Embroider satin stitch marking on the hindwings.

Embroider two or three short stitches for each spot over the wings of the white ermine moth using C.

Place the forewings on top of hindwings in the desired position and use the tails of yarn to sew the top edges together where they will be joined to the body.

Sew the wings to the top of the body, underneath the thorax, stitching neatly around the tops to attach them securely. Sew a stitch from the lower end of each hindwing through the body to hold them in place. Sew the side and lower edges of the thorax in place over the wings and body.

Weave in all the yarn ends.

Stag beetle

The legs, mandibles and antennae are all made using a wire structure. The mandibles are crocheted, whereas the wire of the legs and antennae are wrapped in crochet and embroidery threads, creating various finishes.

Materials

- Anchor Freccia, 100% cotton (311yd/285m per 50g ball):
  1 x 50g ball in 0641 (A)
  1 x 50g ball in 0044 (B)
  59in (150cm) length in 0320 (C)
- 1.75mm (UK2:US6) crochet hook
- Sharp-ended darning needle
- Small amount of toy stuffing
- 6in (15cm) length of 18-gauge (1mm) craft wire for the mandibles
- 3 lengths of 18-gauge (1mm) craft wire, each measuring 5⅛in (13cm), for the legs
- 12in (30cm) length of 26-gauge (0.4mm) craft wire for the antennae
- 3½in (9cm) length of 26-gauge (0.4mm) craft wire for the palps
- Stranded embroidery thread in black
- Clear nylon invisible thread
- 1 pair of ⁵⁄₃₂in (4mm) looped glass teddy bear eyes or beads
- Long-nose pliers
- All-purpose adhesive
- Stitch marker

Size

Approximately 5⅛in (13cm) long, from tip of mandibles to end of body, excluding legs.

Tension

34 sts and 33 rows to 4in (10cm) over double crochet using 1.75mm hook. Use larger or smaller hook if necessary to obtain correct tension.

Method

The stag beetle's abdomen, pronotum and head are crocheted in one piece, in continuous rounds and rows of double crochet. A line of stitches crocheted into unworked loops of a previous round forms an edging at the base of the pronotum and head. The wing cases are worked in rows of double crochet and joined to unworked loops of a previous round on the body by crocheting into each stitch of both pieces at the same time. The mandibles (enlarged mouth parts) are crocheted and sewn together around a length of wire. The legs are made of craft wire wrapped in increasing layers of yarn at different intervals and bent into shape. The antennae and palps are made in the same way and wrapped in embroidery thread. The back loops of the last row of the head are joined to create a straight seam, and then the unworked front loops are crocheted into to form a channel. The antennae and palps are then stitched to the mandibles and the joined pieces are inserted into the channel on top of the head, finished with a crocheted flap that goes over the centre of the mandibles, from the front to the back. Finally, glass eyes or beads are sewn to each side of the head.

1 ch at beg of the row/round does not count as a st throughout.

Body

Abdomen

With 1.75mm hook and A, make a magic loop (see page 127).
Round 1: 1 ch, 5 dc into loop (5 sts).
Round 2 (inc): (Dc2inc) 5 times (10 sts).
Pull tightly on short end of yarn to close loop.
Round 3 (inc): (Dc2inc, 1 dc) 5 times (15 sts).
Round 4 (inc): (Dc2inc, 2 dc) 5 times (20 sts).

Rounds 5–15: 1 dc in each dc. Stuff abdomen before continuing, keeping a flattened shape.
Round 16: Skip next 4 dc, 1 dc in back loop only of next 6 dc, skip next 4 dc, 1 dc in both loops of next 6 dc. Continue on these 12 sts.
Round 17: 1 dc in each dc. Join C in last dc. Carry unused yarn on WS of work.
Round 18: 1 dc in each dc with C. Turn at end of last round. Do not fasten off.

Pronotum

The following is worked in rows.
Row 1 (WS) (inc): With A, 1 ch, (dc2inc, 1 dc, dc2inc) 4 times, turn (20 sts).
Row 2 (RS): 1 ch, 1 dc in back loop only of each dc, turn.
Row 3: 1 ch, 1 dc in each dc, turn.
Row 4 (dec): With C, 1 ch, (3 dc, dc2tog twice, 3 dc) twice, turn (16 sts).
Do not fasten off.

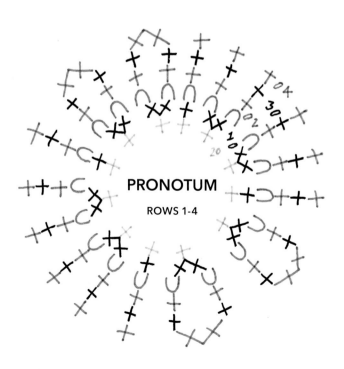

PRONOTUM

ROWS 1-4

ABDOMEN
ROUNDS 1-18

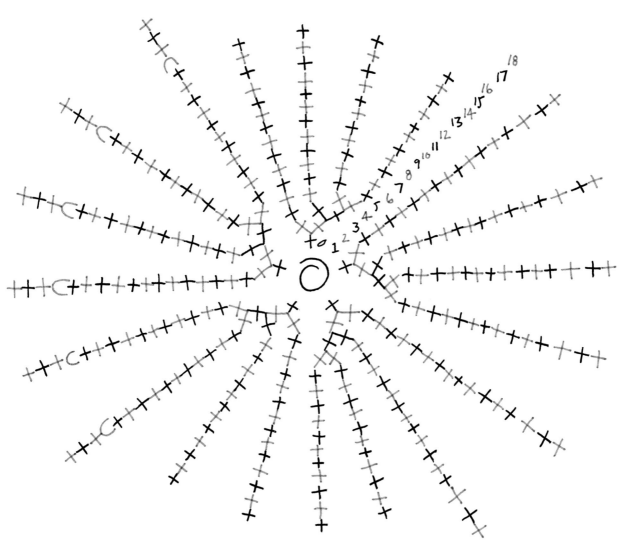

Key

↺ Magic loop		⤬⤮⤬ dc3inc	
⟋ Chain (ch)		T Half treble (htr)	
• Slip stitch (sl st)		ⅎ Treble (tr)	
+ Double crochet (dc)		∩ work into back loop only	
⤬⤮ dc2inc		∪ work into front loop only	
⤬⤬ dc2tog			

Head

Row 1 (WS): 1 ch, 1 dc in each dc with A, turn.
Row 2 (RS) (inc): 1 ch, (dc2inc, 2 dc, dc2inc) 4 times in back loops only, turn (24 sts).
Rows 3–5: 1 ch, dc in each dc, turn. Do not fasten off.

Join edges

Next: Flatten the end with WS together. Make 1 ch, sl st into back loop only of next 12 sts on both sides at the same time to join. Do not fasten off.

Shape top head

Next row (RS): Starting on opposite side to open edges of head, 1 ch, 1 dc in each of the next 24 unworked front loops of row 5, place marker in 20th st, sl st to first dc. Fasten off.

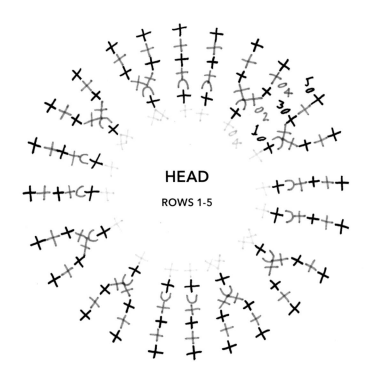

HEAD

ROWS 1-5

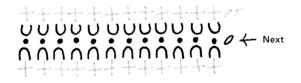

JOIN EDGES

← Next

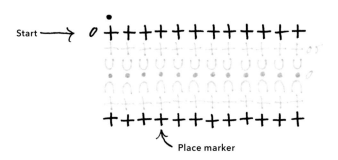

SHAPE TOP HEAD

Start →

Place marker

Shape front head

With 1.75mm hook and WS of previous row facing, skip last 4 sts worked and rejoin A with a sl st to next dc, indicated by marker.

Row 1 (WS): 1 dc in same st as sl st, 1 dc in next 3 dc, turn (4 sts).

Row 2 (RS) (dec): 1 ch, (skip next dc, 1 dc in next dc) twice, turn (2 sts).

Row 3 (inc): 1 ch, (dc2inc) twice (4 sts).

Fasten off, leaving a long tail of thread.

Head edging

Next: With head facing upwards, 1.75mm hook and A, sl st in first of 16 unworked front loops of row 1 of head, 1 dc in same st as sl st, (1 htr, 1 tr) in next st, 1 htr in next st, sl st in next 2 sts, 1 htr in next st, (1 tr, 1 htr) in next st, 1 dc in next 9 sts (18 sts).

Fasten off, leaving a long tail of thread.

SHAPE FRONT HEAD

ROWS 1-3

HEAD EDGING

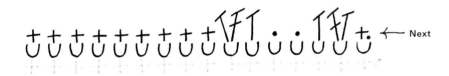

Pronotum edging

Next: With head facing upwards, 1.75mm hook and A, sl st in first of 20 unworked front loops of row 1 of pronotum; beg in same st as sl st, 1 dc in next 20 sts.
Fasten off, leaving a long tail of thread.

Elytra

(wing cases) (make 2)

With 1.75mm hook and B, make 12 ch.
Row 1 (RS): 1 dc in 2nd ch from hook, 1 dc in next 9 ch, 3 dc in end ch, 1 dc in reverse side of next 10 ch, turn (23 sts).
Row 2 (WS) (inc): 1 ch, 1 dc in next 11 dc, dc3inc, 1 dc in next 11 dc, turn (25 sts).
Row 3 (inc): 1 ch, 1 dc in next 12 dc, dc3inc, 1 dc in next 12 dc (27 sts).
Fasten off.
Do not fasten off the second elytra.
Next (RS): Rotate the elytra and work 5 dc evenly along edge of rows, with RS of first elytra facing, work 5 dc evenly along the edge to join.
Do not fasten off.

PRONOTUM EDGING

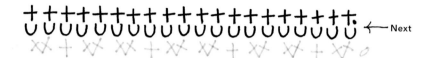

ELYTRA

ROWS 1-3

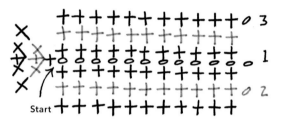

ELYTRA CONTINUED

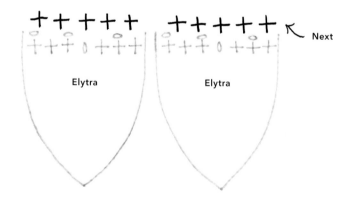

Elytra   Elytra

118

Join elytra to body

Next: With head facing downwards and tips of elytra pointing up, place WS of elytra, on RS of body, aligning the 10 sts at the edge with the 6 unworked front loops of round 15 of abdomen and 2 skipped sts on each side. Inserting hook into front loop only of each skipped st and unworked loops of round 15 first, and then the corresponding st of the elytra, work 1 dc in next 10 sts at same time to join. Fasten off, leaving a long tail of thread.

JOIN ELYTRA TO BODY

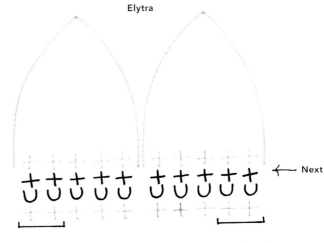

Elytra

← Next

Skipped stitches   Skipped stitches

Mandibles

With 1.75mm hook and B,
make 51 ch.
Row 1 (WS): Beg in 2nd ch from
hook, *1 dc in next 5 ch; 4 ch, 1 dc in
2nd ch from hook, 1 dc in next 2 ch to
make branch, 1 dc in next 8 ch;
3 ch, 1 dc in 2nd ch from hook, 1 dc
in next ch to make branch; 1 dc in
next 2 ch, 1 htr in next 20 ch, 1 dc
in next 2 ch, 3 ch, 1 dc in 2nd ch
from hook, 1 dc in next ch to make
branch; 1 dc in next 8 ch; 4 ch,
1 dc in 2nd ch from hook, 1 dc in next
2 ch to make branch; 1 dc in next 5
ch; rep from * in reverse side of next
50 ch.
Fasten off, leaving a long tail of thread.

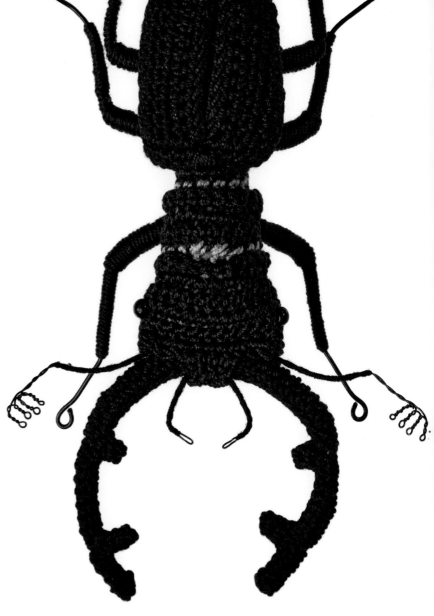

MANDIBLES

ROW 1

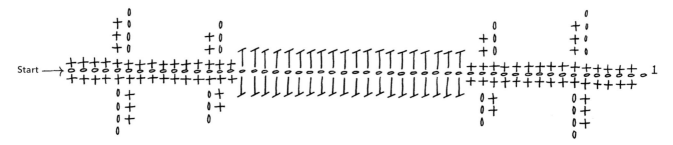

Making up

Body

Stuff the rest of the body and head through an opening in the side, keeping a flattened shape. Sew together the opening at the side of the head. Align the two unworked stitches on each side of the openings on round 16 of abdomen and sew together the back loops. Use the tails of thread to sew ends of edging together at the base of the head and pronotum. Use the tail of thread left after joining the elytra to the body to sew them to the surface of the abdomen. Embroider the scutellum, the triangular section at the top of the wing cases, in satin stitch (see page 133) with A.

Legs

Use pliers to bend approximately ¼in (6mm) into a loop at each end of the wire. Starting at the centre of the wire, wind A tightly around the wire, working over the thread end, to within ⅝in (1.5cm) from the end. Wind a second layer in the opposite direction back over the wrapped wire to the centre. Wrap a third layer of thread from the centre to within 1⅜in (3.5cm) of the end, then repeat in the opposite direction to cover the last section with a fourth layer, finishing in the centre. Turn the wire and repeat to cover the other side. Trim the excess thread and secure the end of the thread with a dab of all-purpose adhesive and allow to dry. Make two bends in the covered wire, ⅝in (1.5cm) and 1⅜in (3.5cm) from each end to shape the legs. Sew to the base of the body using A.

Mandibles

Use pliers to bend under approximately ¼in (6mm) at each end of the wire. Lay the wire down the centre of the WS of the mandible. With the tail of yarn left after fastening off, sew the stitches on each side together, encasing the wire.

Antennae

With pliers, make a bend 2in (5cm) from the end of the wire. To make the comb shape, make seven bends, back and forth, at ¼in (6mm) intervals and twist together. Repeat to shape the other end of the wire. Twist the lengths of wire left at each end around the wire between the combs. Starting ⅝in (1.5cm) from the top of the comb on the antennae, wrap two strands of embroidery thread around the wire and over the thread end to the centre of the wire, take the threads up to ⅝in (1.5cm) from the top of the other comb end and wrap them tightly around the wire and thread, finishing at the centre. Apply a dab of all-purpose adhesive to secure the ends and allow to dry. Sew to the lower edge of the centre of the mandibles using two strands of embroidery thread.

Palps

Follow the instructions for the antennae instructions on page 135 to make the palps. Wrap the wire in two strands of black embroidery thread. Sew to the centre of the top of the mandibles using the same thread.

Finish head

Place the mandibles, with attached antennae and palps, inside the last row of stitches at the top of the head. Wrap the front head piece over the centre of the mandibles and sew the four stitches of the last row to the four central stitches at the back of the head with the tail of thread left after fastening off. Sew a few stitches through all crocheted layers, from the back to the front of the last row of the head, to hold the mandibles in position. Make a ⅝in (1.5cm) bend at the end of each antenna. Curve the antennae from the centre to shape them. Make a ¼in (6mm) bend at the end of each palp. Bend the palps up from the centre.

Eyes

Attach the glass eyes or beads using invisible nylon thread (see page 135).

Weave in all the thread ends.

Techniques

Getting started

Everything you need to make your minibeast is listed at the beginning of each pattern. Here you will find more information on getting started.

Hooks

Crochet hook sizes vary widely, from tiny hooks that produce a very fine stitch when used with threads, to oversized hooks for working with several strands of yarn at one time to create a bulky fabric. Using a larger or smaller hook will change the look of the fabric; it will also affect the tension and the amount of yarn required. The projects in this book use just three sizes, 1.25mm (UK3:US8), 1.50mm (UK2½:US7) and 1.75mm (UK2:US6).

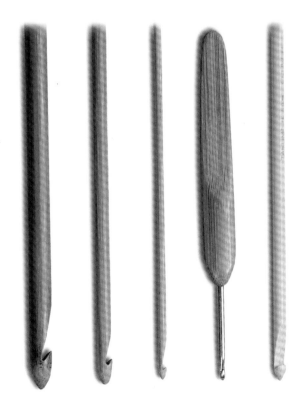

Needles

A blunt-ended yarn needle is used to sew the bumblebees together (see page 31). The large eye makes it easy to thread the needle and the rounded end will prevent any snagging. Use a needle with a sharp point for projects using threads.

Substituting yarns

When substituting yarns or threads, it is important to calculate the number of balls required by the number of yards or metres per ball, rather than the weight of the yarn, because this varies according to the fibre. Tension is also important. Always work a tension swatch in the yarn you wish to use before starting a project.

Reading charts

Each symbol on a chart represents a stitch; each round or row represents one round or row of crochet.

For rounds of crochet, read the chart anti-clockwise, starting at the centre and working out to the last round on the chart.

For rows of crochet, the chart should be read back and forth, following the number at the beginning of each row.

The charts are shown in alternate rounds or rows of blue and black. The last round or row from a previous chart is shown in grey. Where multiple colour changes are used, the stitches on the charts are shown in the colour to represent each yarn.

Tension

It is vital to check your tension before starting a project, as this will affect the size and look of the insect or spider, as well as the amount of yarn you will use. The tension is the number of rows and stitches per square inch or centimetre of crocheted fabric.

Stitches

Using the same size hook and type of stitch as in the pattern, work a sample of around 5in (12.5cm) square and then smooth out on a flat surface. Place a ruler horizontally across the work and mark 4in (10cm) with pins. Count the number of stitches between the pins, including half stitches. This will give you the tension of stitches.

Rows

Measure the tension of rows by placing a ruler vertically over the work and mark 4in (10cm) with pins. Count the number of rows between the pins.

If the number of stitches and rows is greater than those stated in the pattern, your tension is tighter and you should use a larger hook. If the number of stitches and rows is fewer than those stated in the pattern, your tension is looser, so you should use a smaller hook.

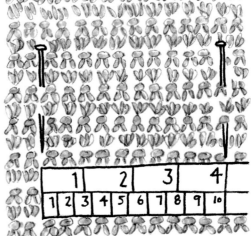

Stitches

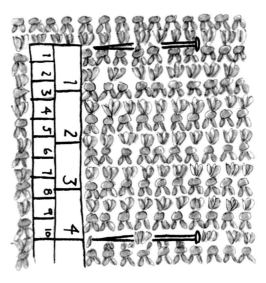

Rows

Crochet stitches

Here you will find the basic information on how to hold the hook and yarn, crocheting the stitches, shaping the pieces and working with multiple colours.

Slip knot

Take the end of the yarn and form it into a loop. Holding it in place between thumb and forefinger, insert the hook through the loop, catch the long end that is attached to the ball, and draw it back through. Keeping the yarn looped on the hook, pull through until the loop closes around the hook, ensuring it is not tight. Pulling on the short end of yarn will loosen the knot, while pulling on the long end will tighten it.

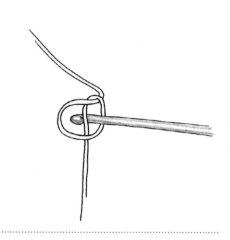

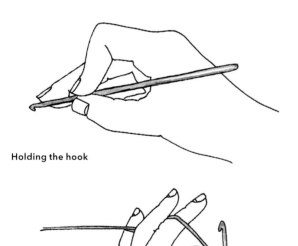

Holding the hook

Holding the yarn

Holding the work

Hook

Hold the hook as you would a pencil, bringing your middle finger forward to rest near the tip of the hook. This will help control the movement of the hook, while the fingers of your other hand will regulate the tension of the yarn. The hook should face you, pointing slightly downwards. The motion of the hook and yarn should be free and even, not tight. This will come with practice.

Yarn

To hold your work and control the tension, pass the yarn over the first two fingers of your left hand (right if you are left-handed), under the third finger and around the little finger, and let the yarn fall loosely to the ball. As you work, take the stitch you made between the thumb and forefinger of the same hand.

The hook is usually inserted through the top two loops of a stitch as you work, unless otherwise stated in a pattern. A different effect is produced when only the back or front loop of the stitch is picked up.

Magic loop

Many of the crocheted pieces start with an adjustable loop of yarn. To make the loop, wind the yarn around a finger, insert the hook, catch the yarn and draw back though the loop. After a couple of rounds have been crocheted, covering the loop of yarn, the short end of yarn is pulled tight to close the centre. An alternative method is to make four chain stitches and then slip stitch to the first chain to form a ring. However, this technique does leave a hole in the middle.

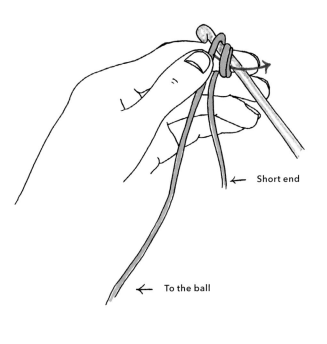

← **Short end**

← **To the ball**

Chain (ch)

1 Pass the hook under and over the yarn that is held taut between the first and second fingers. This is called 'yarn over hook' (yoh), or 'yarn round hook' (yrh). This book uses the former term. Draw the yarn through the loop on the hook. This makes 1 chain (ch).

2 Repeat step 1, keeping the thumb and forefinger of the left hand close to the hook, until you have as many chain stitches as required.

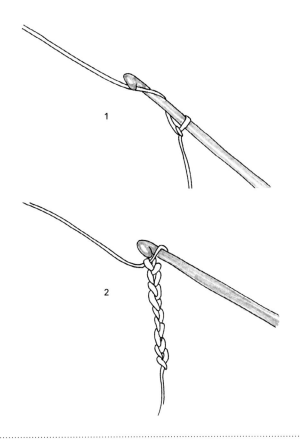

Slip stitch (sl st)

Make a practice chain of 10.

1 Insert hook into first stitch (st), yoh, draw through both loops on hook. This forms 1 slip stitch (sl st).

2 Continue to end. This will give you 10 slip stitches (10 sts).

Double crochet (dc)

Make a practice chain of 17. Skip the first ch.

1 Insert hook from front into the next stitch, yoh and draw back through the stitch (two loops on hook).

2 Yoh and draw through two loops (one loop on hook). This makes 1 double crochet (dc).

Repeat steps 1 and 2 to the end of the row. On the foundation chain of 17 sts, you should have 16 double crochet sts (16 sts).

Next row

Turn the work so the reverse side faces you. Make 1 ch. This is the turning chain; it helps keep a neat edge and does not count as a stitch. Rep steps 1 and 2 to the end of the row. Continue until the desired number of rows is complete. Fasten off.

Fastening off

When you have finished, fasten off by cutting the yarn around 4¾in (12cm) from the work. Draw the loose end through the remaining loop, pulling it tightly.

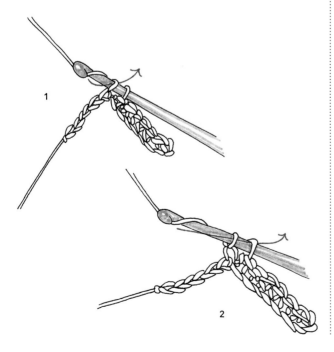

Half treble (htr)

Make a practice chain of 17. Skip the first 2 ch (these count as the first half treble stitch).

1 Yoh, insert hook into the next stitch, yoh and draw back through stitch (three loops on hook).

2 Yoh, draw through all three loops (one loop on hook). This forms 1 half treble (htr).

Repeat steps 1 and 2 to the end of the row. On the foundation chain of 17 sts, you should have 16 half trebles (16 sts), including the 2 ch at the beginning of the row, which is counted as the first stitch.

Next row

Turn the work so the reverse side faces you. Make 2 ch to count as the first half treble. Skip the first stitch of the previous row. Repeat steps 1 and 2 for the next 14 htr of the last row, work 1 htr in the second of the 2 ch at the end of the row. Continue until the desired number of rows is complete. Fasten off.

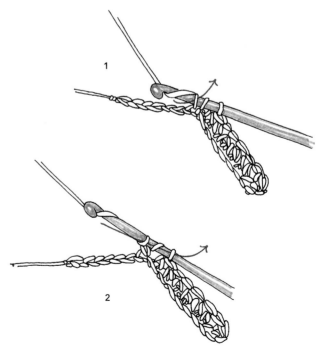

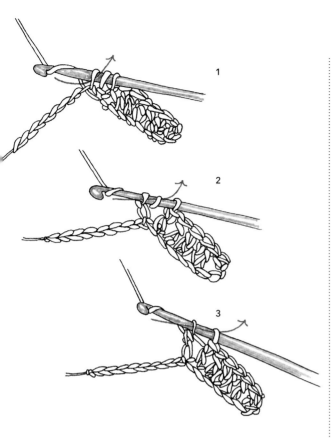

Treble (tr)

Make a practice chain of 18. Skip the first 3 ch (these count as the first treble stitch).

1 Yoh, insert hook into the next stitch, yoh and draw back through the stitch (three loops on hook).

2 Yoh, draw through two loops (two loops on hook).

3 Yoh, draw through two loops (one loop on hook). This forms 1 treble (tr).

Repeat steps 1–3 to end of row. On the foundation chain of 18 sts you should have 16 trebles (16 sts), including the 3 ch at the beginning of the row, which is counted as the first stitch.

Next row

Turn the work so the reverse side faces you. Make 3 ch to count as the first treble. Skip the first stitch of the previous row. Repeat steps 1–3 to the end of the row, working 1 tr into the third of the 3 ch at the beginning of the last row. Continue until the desired number of rows is complete. Fasten off.

Double treble (dtr)

Make a practice chain of 19. Skip the first 4 ch (these count as the first double treble stitch).

1 Yoh twice, insert hook into the next stitch, yoh and draw back through stitch (four loops on hook).

2 (Yoh, draw through two loops) three times (one loop on hook). This forms 1 double treble (dtr).

Repeat steps 1 and 2 to the end of the row. On the foundation chain of 19 sts you should have 16 double trebles (16 sts), including the 4 ch at the beginning of the row, counted as the first stitch.

Next row

Turn the work so the reverse side faces you. Make 4 ch to count as the first double treble. Skip the first stitch of the previous row. Repeat steps 1 and 2 to the end of the row. Continue until you have completed the desired number of rows. Fasten off.

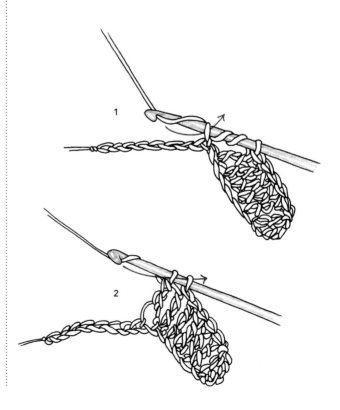

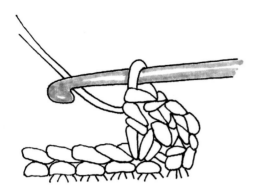

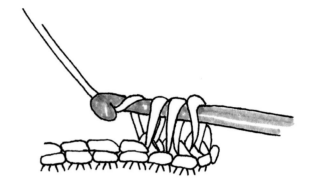

Increasing (inc)

To increase 1 double crochet (dc2inc), half treble (htr2inc) or treble stitch (tr2inc), work two stitches into one stitch of the previous row. To increase 2 double crochet (dc3inc), work three stitches into one stitch of the previous row.

Decreasing (dec)

Decrease 1 double crochet stitch (dc2tog)

1 Insert the hook into the next st, yoh and draw back through the stitch (two loops on hook).

2 Insert the hook into the following st, yoh and draw back through the st (three loops on hook).

3 Yoh and draw through all three loops.

Decrease 1 half treble stitch (htr2tog)

1 Yoh, insert the hook into the next st, yoh and draw back through the stitch (three loops on hook).

2 Yoh, insert the hook into the following st, yoh and draw back through the st (five loops on hook).

3 Yoh and draw through all five loops.

Mirror spider (page 92) and ladybird (page 84).

Crocheting around wire

The last row of some of the wings are crocheted around craft wire so they retain their shape. Follow the instructions and illustration for carrying unused yarn across the back of the work, crocheting over the craft wire with every stitch to enclose it.

Working with multiple colours

Joining a new colour

When joining in a new colour at the beginning of a round or middle of a row, work the last step of the stitch in the new colour. Catch the yarn in the new colour and draw through the loops on the hook to complete the stitch.

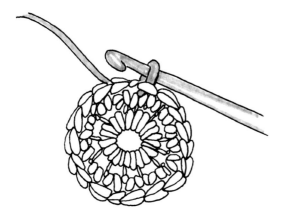

Joining a new colour at the beginning of a round

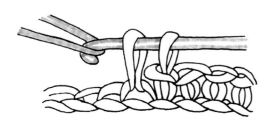

Joining a new colour in the middle of a row

Carrying unused yarn across the work

When the colour that is not in use is to be carried across the wrong side of the work, it can be hidden along the line of stitches being made by working over the unused strand every few stitches with the new colour. When both sides of the work will be visible, the unused strand is worked over on every stitch, keeping the crocheted fabric neat on both sides. Lay the strand not being used on top of the previous row of stitches and crochet over it in the new colour, covering the unused colour. This method is used for the swallowtail butterflies and harnessed tiger moth on pages 60 and 101.

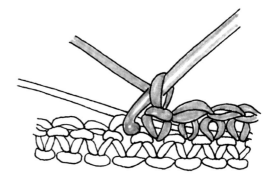

Carrying unused yarn across the work

Working into the back or front loop only

The front loop of a stitch is the one closer to you; the back loop is the stitch further away. Generally, the hook is inserted into both loops of a stitch, but when only one loop is crocheted into, the horizontal bar of the remaining loop is left on the surface of the fabric. This method is used to create the cicada's mesonotum and edging of its protonum (page 37).

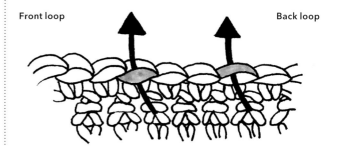

Front loop   Back loop

131

Finishing touches

Glass eyes, beads and some simple embroidery are the final touches used to finish these crocheted creatures, after stuffing and stitching the pieces together.

Stuffing

Polyester stuffing is a synthetic fibre that is lightweight and washable. Pure wool stuffing is a lovely, natural fibre. Durable and soft, it can be washed by hand but cannot be machine washed as it will shrink and felt. Kapok is a natural fibre with a soft, silky texture. It comes from a seedpod that is harvested from the ceiba tree.

Before stuffing, tease the fibres by pulling them apart with your fingers to make them light and fluffy. Use small amounts at a time and line the inside of the crocheted fabric with a layer of stuffing before building up the filling in the centre. This will prevent the crocheted piece from looking lumpy.

Sewing the pieces together

When stitching up your work, use glass-headed dressmaker's pins to hold the pieces together.

Whip stitch

This stitch is used to sew together the edges of the butterfly and moth abdomens (see pages 75 and 111). Thread the tail of yarn left after fastening off onto a darning needle. Insert the needle from back to front through a stitch on both sides at the same time and draw the yarn through the stitch. Insert the needle through the next stitch on both sides from back to front as before and continue to the end. The yarn will be wrapped around the edges, joining the two sides.

Whip stitch

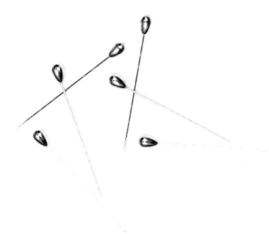

Embroidery stitches

Embroidered stitches add extra detail to a few of the finished projects. The Christmas beetle's elytra are decorated with tiny straight stitches (see page 59) and satin stitch is used for the reflection of light in the dragonfly's eyes (see page 83).

Straight stitch

This is a single stitch that can be worked in varying lengths, useful for embroidering lines.

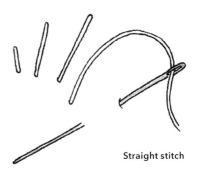

Straight stitch

Back stitch

This is a good method for sewing on the wings. Work close to the edges of the pieces for a neat finish.

Begin by working a couple of stitches over each other to secure the seam. Bring the needle through to the front of the work one stitch ahead of the last stitch made. Then insert the needle back through the work at the end of the last stitch.

Repeat to complete the seam, making sure your stitches are neat.

Satin stitch

Work straight stitches side by side and close together across a shape. Take care to keep the stitches even and the edge neat. The finished result will look like satin.

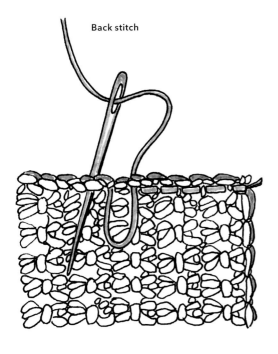

Back stitch

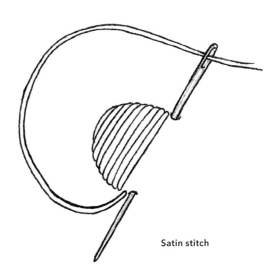

Satin stitch

Fly stitch

A fly stitch is embroidered on the mirror spider (see page 97).

1 Bring the yarn through to the front of the work on the left side of the centre of the stitch and hold it down with your thumb. Insert the needle to the right, in line with the point where it first emerged. Bring the needle back through to the front of the work and a little way up, in line with the centre of the stitch, keeping the yarn under the needle.

2 Insert the needle back into the work to form a V shape with the stitch. Insert the needle lower down, forming a straight line below the V-shaped stitch.

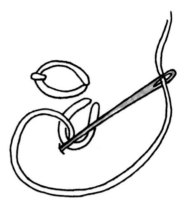

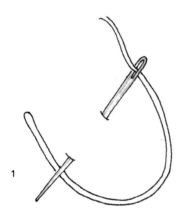

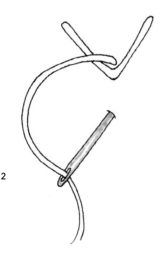

Lazy daisy stitch

This stitch is used on the thorax of the harnessed tiger moth (see page 111). Bring the yarn through to the front of the work at the position where the stitch is to be made, and insert the needle back through at the same point to form a loop. Hold the loop down with your thumb. Bring the needle back through to the front of the work, a little way down according to the length of the stitch you wish to make, keeping the yarn under the needle. Reinsert the needle over the yarn and into the same point it emerged to form a small stitch to anchor the loop.

Fastening off

To fasten off embroidery on the moth's wings, run the yarn along the line of stitches on the wrong side of the work. A small knot can be made to keep the stitches secure, so it won't form a visible lump at the front of the crocheted fabric. Cut the end of the yarn.

To fasten off embroidery on the head or body of a bug, thread the yarn through to an area of the same colour where it won't show and make a small knot, pulling it tightly so it disappears inside the crocheted piece. Weave in the ends of yarn.

Antennae

Most of the antennae are made using wire that is wrapped in yarn or thread. Some of the insects' legs are made in the same way. Choose a wire that is not too soft, as it could break if overworked.

Materials

- See pattern for specified yarn/thread and length of wire required
- Long-nose pliers
- All-purpose adhesive

1 Use the pliers to bend the ends of the wire so it is double thickness and the ends meet in the middle. Twist each side of the doubled wire together.

2 Wind the yarn around the twisted wire, starting at the tip of one antenna and working over the end of the yarn to the middle. Take the yarn to the tip of the other antenna and wrap it evenly and tightly back along the length, finishing at the middle. Trim the excess yarn. Secure the end of the yarn with a dab of all-purpose adhesive and allow to dry. Use the specified yarn or thread to sew a few stitches through the head and over the centre of the covered wire to attach the antennae. Bend the antennae into shape.

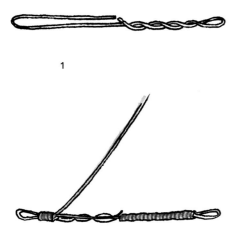

Eyes

Glass teddy bear eyes, beads and embroidery are used for the eyes on these projects. If using glass eyes with wire loops, use a needle to make a hole where the eyes will be, as this will make it easier to insert the wire loop.

Attaching glass teddy bear eyes or beads

1 Cut a 15¾in (40cm) length of clear nylon invisible thread. Double the thread and pass both loose ends through the wire loop of the glass eye or the hole in the bead.

2 Thread both the ends of thread onto a needle and insert the needle into the head at the position of the eye, right through to the base of the bug, so the needle emerges between the stitches. Leave the ends of the thread of the first eye hanging at the point where they emerged. Attach the second eye in the same way, pulling the threads through, close to the threads of the first eye.

3 Remove the needle and check the position of the eyes. Tie the threads together, knotting them securely. Thread all the strands onto the needle and pull them through to the inside of the bug to hide the ends. Trim the excess ends that poke out of the bug.

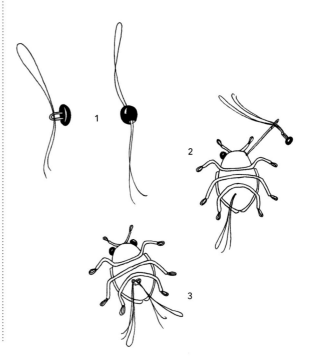

Display & care

After making these projects, you might want to hang a butterfly in a picture frame, turn a beetle into an accessory, or leave them just as they are. Here are some tips on how to display the finished pieces.

Picture frame

Materials

- Box frame, deep enough to fit the project
- Mount board to fit frame
- Sharp needle
- Clear invisible nylon thread

Mark the position of the project on the back of the mount board. Poke two holes through the centre, approximately ⅝in (1.5cm) apart, to attach the piece. Thread the invisible thread through the base of the insect and pass each end through the holes, from the front to the back, of the mount board. Knot the ends of the thread together. Place in frame and reassemble. To frame taller creatures, such as the mirror spider, attach them to the mount board with invisible thread through the loops of wire at the end of the legs.

Christmas beetle (page 52)

Brooch

Materials

- Brooch bar
- Needle
- Clear invisible nylon thread

Position the clasp on the base of the insect so the antennae or legs won't get knocked out of shape or damaged when fastening the brooch. Sew the brooch bar to the crocheted base of the insect, avoiding the legs, using invisible thread. Sew four or five stitches through each hole on both sides, or around the bar if there are no holes.

Glass dome

Materials

- Glass dome measuring approximately 4in (10cm) in diameter for small projects and 5½in (14cm) in diameter for large projects
- 18-gauge (1mm) florist or sugarcraft wire
- Sharp-ended darning needle
- Drill
- Long-nose pliers
- Superglue

Poke a sharp-ended darning needle between the stitches and into the stuffing of the crocheted insect to create a channel for the wire. Push the wire inside the insect. Drill a hole in the centre of the base of the dome for the other end of the wire. Use the pliers to cut the wire to the length required to fit inside the dome, allowing for the depth of the hole in the base. Apply some superglue to the end of the wire before inserting it into the drilled hole. Place the dome on the base.

Moths (page 98)

Caring for your miniature beasts

As with all decorations, these small pieces will accumulate dust and may need a bit of care every so often to keep them looking as good as new.

Use a soft brush to remove surface dust. It is best to avoid firm bristles as they may snag the fibres of the yarn. A piece of fabric with a pile, such as velvet, can also be used. The direction of the pile can be found by brushing your hand over the material. One way will feel smooth, whereas brushing in the opposite direction will feel rough. Brush the rough side of the pile across the crocheted bug to remove dust. Be careful with wire, particularly in the antennae and legs, as bending and reshaping them too often can cause the wire to snap.

Abbreviations

ch chain
cm centimetre(s)
dc double crochet
dc2inc work 2 double crochet stitches into the next stitch to increase
dc2tog work 2 double crochet stitches together to decrease
dc3inc work 3 double crochet stitches into the next stitch to increase
dec decrease
dtr double treble

dtr2inc work 2 double treble stitches into the next stitch to increase
htr half treble
htr2inc work 2 half treble stitches into the next stitch to increase
htr2tog work 2 half treble stitches together to decrease
in inches
inc increase
lp(s) loop(s)
m metre(s)
mm millimetre(s)

rep repeat
RS right side
sl st slip stitch
sp space
st(s) stitch(es)
tog together
tr treble
tr2inc work 2 half treble stitches into the next stitch to increase
WS wrong side
yd yards
yoh yarn over hook

Instructions
cluster yoh, insert hook into next st, yoh, draw back through st, yoh, draw through 2 loops on hook, (yoh, insert hook in same st, yoh, draw back through st, yoh, draw through 2 loops on hook) twice, yoh, draw through all 4 loops.

2-htr puff yoh, insert hook into next st, yoh, draw back through st; yoh, insert hook into same st, yoh, draw back through st, yoh, draw through all 5 loops.

3-htr puff yoh, insert hook into next st, yoh, draw back through st, (yoh, insert hook in same st, yoh, draw back through st) twice, yoh, draw through all 7 loops.

*/**/*** work instructions following the asterisks, repeating them as many times as directed.

() repeat instructions inside brackets as many times as directed.

Conversions

Steel crochet hooks
UK	Metric	US
6	0.60mm	14
5½	–	13
5	0.75mm	12
4½	–	11
4	1.00mm	10
3½	–	9
3	1.25mm	8
2½	1.50mm	7
2	1.75mm	6
1½	–	5

Standard crochet hooks
UK	Metric	US
14	2mm	–
13	2.25mm	B/1
12	2.5mm	–
–	2.75mm	C/2
11	3mm	–
10	3.25mm	D/3
9	3.5mm	E/4
–	3.75mm	F/5
8	4mm	G/6
7	4.5mm	7

UK	Metric	US
6	5mm	H/8
5	5.5mm	I/9
4	6mm	J/10
3	6.5mm	K/10.5
2	7mm	–
0	8mm	L/11
00	9mm	M–N/13
000	10mm	N–P/15

UK/US crochet terms
UK	US
Double crochet	Single crochet
Half treble	Half double crochet
Treble	Double crochet
Double treble	Treble crochet

Note: This book uses UK crochet techniques

Suppliers

Yarn/ crochet thread

Germany

Rico Design
GmbH & Co. KG
Industriestr. 19–23
33034 Brakel
Tel: +49 (0)52 72 602 0
e: info@rico-design.de
www.rico-design.de

Norway

Drops Design
Drops Design A/S,
Jerikoveien 10 A
1067 Oslo
Tel: +47 23 30 32 20
www.garnstudio.com

The Netherlands

Scheepjes
Mercuriusweg 16
9482 WL Tynaarlo
e: contact@scheepjes.com
www.scheepjes.com

UK

Deramores
Unit 1, Sabre Way
Peterborough
Cambridgeshire
PE1 5EJ
Tel: +44 (0)1733 777345
www.deramores.com

Wool Warehouse
12 Longfield Road
Sydenham Industrial
Estate, Leamington Spa
Warwickshire
CV31 1XB
Tel: +44 (0)1926 882818
sales@woolwarehouse.co.uk
www.woolwarehouse.co.uk

Haberdashery

UK

The Stitchery
12–14 Riverside, High
Street, Lewes, East Sussex
BN7 2RE
Tel: +44 (0)1273 473577
e: info@the-stitchery.co.uk
www.the-stitchery.co.uk

USA

Purl Soho
459 Broome Street
New York, NY 10013
Tel: +1 800 597 7875
e: customerservice@
   purlsoho.com
www.purlsoho.com

Toy stuffing

UK

Deramores
(see Yarn/crochet thread)

Wool Warehouse
(see Yarn/crochet thread)

World of Wool
Unit 8, The Old Railway
Goods Yard, Scar Lane
Milnsbridge, Huddersfield
West Yorkshire
HD3 4PE
Tel: +44 (0)3300 564888
e: info@worldofwool.co.uk
www.worldofwool.co.uk

USA

Purl Soho *(see Haberdashery)*

Craft wire & beads

UK

Beads and More Ltd
1 Elm Grove
Lower Swainswick
Bath, Somerset
BA1 7AZ
www.beadsandmore.co.uk

The Bead Shop Ltd
Granmore Building
186 Cheetham Hill Road
Manchester M8 8LW
Tel: +44 (0)161 274 4040
e: sales@the-beadshop.co.uk
www.the-beadshop.co.uk

Beads Unlimited
Unit 26, Mackley Industrial
Estate, Henfield Road
Small Dole, Henfield
West Sussex BN5 9XR
Tel: +44 (0)1273 740777
www.beadsunlimited.co.uk

Sequins

UK

Sequin World
www.sequinworld.co.uk

Glass eyes

UK

Bear Basics
Tel: +44 (0)1963 34500
www.bearbasics.co.uk

**Mohair Bear Making
Supplies Ltd**
Unit 3, Horton Court
Hortonwood 50
Telford, Shropshire
TF1 7GY
Tel: +44 (0)1952 604096
e: sales@mohairbear
   makingsupplies.co.uk
www.mohairbearmaking
   supplies.co.uk

USA

GlassEyesOnline.com
1283 Sea Island Parkway
St Helena Island
SC 29920
e: info@glasseyesonline.
com
www.glasseyesonline.com

Acknowledgements

I was inspired to design these pieces quite a long time ago and was so excited when I eventually sat down to start this project. Thank you very much Jonathan Bailey for turning my dream of crocheted creatures into a lovely book! Thank you Wendy McAngus, Emma Foster and everyone at GMC, Wayne Blades, Robin Pridy and Neal Grundy, and to Jude Roust. As always, love and hugs to my family for being there, giving me encouragement and their honest opinions on the size of an abdomen or position of compound eyes. I dedicate this book to beautiful Dolly and Winter who are always so enthusiastic about what I am making and say such lovely things about them, and to gorgeous Leo who is the only person I know who absolutely loves spiders!

About the author

Vanessa Mooncie is a contemporary craftsperson, artist and author. She studied fashion and textile design and has worked as a children's wear designer, illustrator and interior designer. More about Vanessa's work can be found at www.vanessamooncie.com. She lives with her family in a rural village in the south of England. Vanessa has written several other titles published by GMC Publications, including *Animal Hats*, *Crocheted Wild Animals*, *Sewn Animal Heads*, *Crocheted Dogs* and *Crocheted Animal Rugs*.

Index

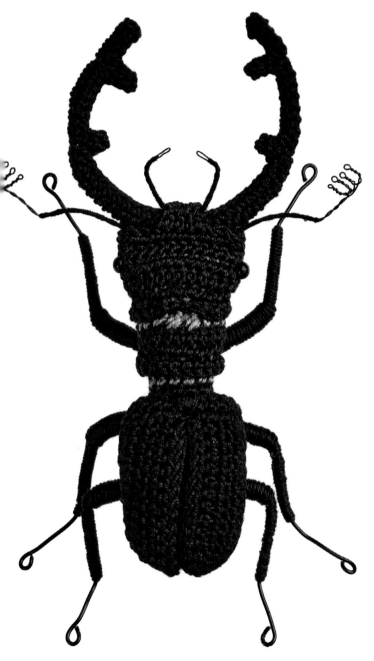

First published 2022 by
Guild of Master Craftsman Publications Ltd,
Castle Place, 166 High Street, Lewes, East Sussex,
BN7 1XU, UK.

Reprinted 2023, 2024

Text and designs © Vanessa Mooncie, 2022

Copyright in the Work © GMC Publications Ltd, 2022

ISBN 978 1 78494 635 7

publisher: Jonathan Bailey
production director: Jim Bulley
editor: Robin Pridy
design & art direction: Wayne Blades
photographer: Neal Grundy
pattern checking: Jude Roust
illustrations & charts: Vanessa Mooncie

Colour origination by GMC Reprographics

Printed and bound in China

To place an order, contact:

GMC Publications Ltd
Castle Place, 166 High Street,
Lewes, East Sussex,
BN7 1XU
United Kingdom
Tel: +44 (0)1273 488005
www.gmcbooks.com